RANDOM WORDS

IVOR BROWN

RANDOM:
'Made, done or occurring at haphazard.'
Oxford English Dictionary

THE BODLEY HEAD

LONDON SYDNEY

TORONTO

© Ivor Brown 1971
ISBN 0 370 01354 9
Printed and bound in Great Britain for
The Bodley Head Ltd
9 Bow Street, London WC2E 7AL
by Richard Clay (The Chaucer Press) Ltd
Bungay, Suffolk
Set in Linotype Baskerville
First published 1971

I am grateful to the following for their letters of encouragement and instruction, and apologise for omitting several whose signatures I cannot decipher.

Jay Ames
A. Oswald Baxter
Theodore L. Bailey
Clare Bennett
Reginald Bosley
Sir Douglas Busk
Norman Collins
Norman Creighton
Alan Dent
Dame Daphne du Maurier
Sir Bernard Fergusson
Professor S. K. Ghosh
Bernard Grebanier
Mrs Prudence Hannay
Sir Rupert Hart-Davis
T. Heron

Walter Humphries
Robin Jenks
Sir Philip Jones
Sir Alan Lascelles
Miss C. E. Mander
Mrs Lucille Moore
Professor Ivan Morris
Eric Partridge
J. B. Priestley
George Richards
Derek Roberts
The Rev J. A. Rosie
H. T. Stables
R. E. Threlfall
P. H. Woods
F. W. Young

Foreword

My excuse for adding yet again to my series of Word
Books must include a confession of self-indulgence.
After reading with enjoyment a book or a passage
in a book I enjoy turning over in my mind or
flavouring on my lips the aspect and sounds which
have given me pleasure because they have conveyed
the thoughts and feelings of the writer with clarity
and cogency. 'Proper words in proper places' was
Swift's definition of literary style. The delight is en-
hanced if assonance is added to propriety and meaning has been blended with the verbal music in which
the English language happily abounds. Having time
on my hands and less mobility in my legs than I, once
fond of walking, would like, I cosset my desk-bound
self with recording for my own satisfaction the
pleasure gained by wondering about the history of
words and the curious ways in which poetry can raise
them to a higher power. Any lover of the good must
resent the bad. So I include some nagging at the
coarse or cloudy misuse of our language. Selfishness
again. Scolds enjoy scolding. In short I am an incurable scribbler, and have no shame in admitting my
surrender to the malady of writer's itch.

I have been fortunate in the assistance of kindly
publishers who have been ready to print with small
profit and I hope without loss these meditations of a
verbal collector which have been spread over thirty
years. My new title was partly suggested by the *Ran-*

dom House Dictionary, as vast in size as rich in information. Random also applies to my meandering in the world of words and to the range of my subject. The British have been random wanderers about the globe and it has been pleasant to know that my ploy is shared by a number of people who, living far away from Britain, remain closely and affectionately interested in the speech, vocabulary and dialects which the English, Scots, Welsh and Irish still use at home and have carried with them in their dispersion.

I am most grateful to those, earlier mentioned by name, who have sent me suggestions and corrections from places as far apart as Canada, the United States, India, Australia and New Zealand. I hopefully await communications from Polynesia to Venezuela and from Antarctica to Spitzbergen. My readers are not to be counted in myriads but they are as widely separated in their homes as they are united in sharing my taste. I have confessed to self-indulgence and now plead guilty to the vanity of one who receives friendly and sometimes flattering letters. He is usually a liar who says that he hates flattery.

The writing to be found in my daily reading seems to improve when it is aimed at the greatest number. The old, turgid journalese has withered away. Newsprint is now vastly expensive. It cost eight pounds a ton in 1939 and now seventy. There must be no waste of paper when the daily printing order runs into several millions. Therefore there must be no waste of words. In the popular press, which is distinguished from the quality press in discussions about journalism, the reporting of events and statement of views must be prompt, precise and clear. The discipline is salutary. There is no waffling.

On the other hand academic English, especially when it emerges from a university's school of sociology, gets more sticky and more stodgy. That I have found to be especially annoying in the frequent re-

8

ports issued after extensive social research. These inquiries into an industry or a social class are incessant, elaborate and expensive. This is part of the Higher Education whose cost to the tax-payer continually soars. A group of students, sociologically orientated, as they would probably call themselves, set out to discover by prolonged inquiry what a practical journalist could discover single-handed in a day or two. The facts and figures of public tastes and habits, the 'whole spectrum of behavioural patterns', in the jargon of the sociologists, are collected by the diligent investigators in factories and homes. Then they are pondered over for the production of a report.

This is compiled in great solemnity and sometimes produces a verbal fog which fully deserves the Johnsonian adjective inspissated. A question is posed. Does our massed society need variety of interests and occupations? Of course it does, you say. But there must be research in depth. When the sociological expert and his underlings have investigated the obvious he pronounces the verdict. After one such 'quiz', involving interviews with a hundred and seventy members of different political parties in one constituency, this was the wisdom acquired and this the way of announcing it:

> The immediate relevance of the theory of mass society here is the postulate that participation in secondary associations, including political and non-political voluntary associations, is functional for the social integration and maintenance of a pluralist democratic society.

I do not think that the author of this ever had or would find employment in a newspaper office. He would have learned better there. Fleet Street once had its Demon Barber in the fictional person of Sweeny Todd. Its occupants are still expert cutters and know how to give verbosity a close shave.

The avoidance of wordiness and woolliness is excellent, but the rejection of writing with a full vocabulary can be a deprivation. This has happened in the theatre. Hilary Spurling, the dramatic critic of the *Spectator*, was making a good point when she said, 'The history of recent English "serious drama" may be seen as a hopeless attempt to reconcile the vehemence of the emotions with the triteness of the language.' John Osborne has given his angry characters speeches with volume and vehemence; but usually in a play of the 'social protest' kind the conflict of opinion is carried on in the small change of drab dialogue. The actor, it is sadly true, is encouraged to be a mutterer by the bad habit of regarding speaking out and speaking up as 'ham'. If he can and does project his voice he is not provided with the properly detonating projectile.

One of the profession who knows how to attack the audience has told me of his delight in being cast in a new production of an old Shaw play. Here were lines with pith and power in them. At last he had something worth saying, commanding attention and demanding a considered and compelling delivery. That the public is aware of this is shown by the frequency and popularity of the revivals in which Shaw business competes surprisingly with show business. The once advanced opinions have become familiar but to hear the English language in full flow is now a rare and an exciting experience.

Journalists rightly insist upon the importance, the duties and the rights of their profession. But they, like the playwrights and the players, have a corner in the vast industry of entertainment. They must amuse as well as instruct. Editors are keen to employ the shrewd and gifted cartoonist. In the Jester's Corner J. B. Morton, D. B. Wyndham Lewis in their 'Populars' and now 'Peter Simple' in the *Daily Telegraph* have mocked in their various ways the fads and follies of the time. The reader who laughed with the Fleet Street clown was also encouraged to smile at the urbane wit and felicity of style to be found in a leading article on one of the lighter topics or in a criticism of the arts. A. B. Walkley of *The Times* and C. E. Montague in the *Manchester Guardian* delighted as well as instructed my years of apprenticeship in their craft. Whether or not the reader was interested in the subject of their comment, possibly a play which few would ever see or a book which few would ever read, he was richly entertained by masters of English prose.

The Third or Fourth Leaders in *The Times* were anonymous but I could assign their authorship on internal evidence. Here surely, with its Dickens quotation, was Bernard Darwin, as responsive to the many pleasures of life as to the comedies, ardours and endurances of the golf course. Here, I was convinced, was the urbane wit and deft touch of Peter Fleming. The weekly reviews were opened by me with the knowledge that the art of essay was alive and smiling. Here, much earlier, was Max Beerbohm, following Bernard Shaw in the *Saturday Review*; here later James Agate, J. B. Priestley and in the *New Statesman* Robert Lynd, who signed himself as 'Y.Y.', all excellent in their qualities. They were like friends who enter the room with a light in their eyes and raise the temperature. Men of letters without being mandarins, they knew how to choose the right word and use it in their affable, engaging prose.

Belles Lettres has become a term of contempt. There was a cause for that. To be an essayist could be thought too easy for one who had the trick of it. With a regular assignment he could become casual; he might have little to say and rely on familiar gambits. There was some mixture of armchair chat with verbal decoration. The horrid word embellishment could be applied to the products of the minor practitioners. Not long ago publishers included in their catalogues a series of books labelled Belles Lettres along with the usual sections of Fiction, History and Biography. One never sees that now.

The Times dropped its essay-type last Leader when it was successfully seeking and obtaining a much larger circulation. That the change was part of the cause cannot be proved, but it may have helped. The weekly reviews discarded the more personal and less factual kind of middle article. The essay, once a mallard of attractive plumage, was a dead duck. America never liked it. The British editors do not want it. The publishers who were ready to print small volumes of collected pieces will not touch them now. There has been a welcome exception in the case of Priestley whose large collection of *Essays of Five Decades* was published both in London and New York in 1958. He always had matter for his brief discourse: there was salt as well as sweetness when he wrote of his 'Delights'. He was never whimsical or mannered. He wrote exemplary English.

Journalism increasingly prefers fact to fancy and statistical reports to colourful reporting. The essayist who caught the life and mood, the humours and the habits of a sea-side or popular 'resort' perhaps to perfection, in fifteen hundred words has been replaced by the News Team which questions hundreds of the inhabitants and produces a documented account of the hotels and the visitors, the lodgings and the tastes of the lodgers, the Town Council and its plans for the inflow of tourists and the outflow of sewage. The information is ample but the result has a Blue Book quality. A single good reporter of the old school caught the essence and the atmosphere of a place in a random way and he was far more readable. A well-worded paragraph can say more than a pile of figures.

In recording and partly regretting the trend in journalism which has diminished both vocabulary and personality in the description of events I must confess my interest. In the lingo of Whitehall I am a redundant essayist seeking redeployment. When I was writing for the *Saturday* and *Week-end Reviews* and weekly essays for the *Manchester Guardian* and the *Observer* in their old forms I was, I suppose, in the Belle-Lettrist class and my bits and pieces were accepted by publishers for later reprinting in that category. The now despicable essayist is still inside me. Hence it will be seen by readers of my previous Word Books that I have included fewer items for comment and expanded what a comedian, interrupting the 'lyric' of his comic song, calls the patter. I do not think the charge of Belle-Lettrism necessarily damning. At least my book is slim and those who can get as far as my note on Prolix will realise that I know the danger of pattering on. This may be the last of my random ramblings in the landscape of vocabulary. But I have made that pledge before and shall not add to the pie-crust of my promises.

A

Abhominable

I like to find the spelling of abhominable and ab-
hominate as one does in the First Folio of Shakespeare. Few subsequent editors have retained the old
form which explains the word's origin and keeps
the suggestion of severance from human nature and
humanity. We cannot know whether the actors of
the period pronounced the h. They were losing something if they dropped it.

The Duke in *Measure for Measure* rebukes Elbow
for the 'abhominable and beastly touches' in his
bawdy-house and bids him 'Go mend, go mend'.
Mending the word has weakened it. The conduct of
'th' adulterous Antony ... most large in his abhom-
inations', is attacked by Maecenas when he is denouncing Cleopatra's lover for giving 'his potent
Regiment to a Trull'. It is curious how the capital
letters give force to the noun. A Trull seems to be
more sluttish than a trull.

Nobody could want Abhorson, the executioner in
'Measure for Measure', to become Aborson in script
or speech. There is some vagueness about the man's
methods since there is almost simultaneous mention
of a rope and an axe. Either way his trade or mystery
is abhorrent. He is one of Shakespeare's best-named
characters, a whoreson dog with the 'ab' suggesting

that he is the son of another such. This links him with the Sergeant Major's Uzzard discussed later on under that title. Surely no actor would reduce him to Aborson which equates him with a surgeon engaged on a now widely permissible operation. Abhorson's profession or 'mystery' as he prefers to call it, needs the 'h' as much as does abhominable.

Accipitrine

The birds in the air have for some time been either swooping or cooing in the vocabulary of politicians and soldiers. In Washington the most militant have been hawks and the less aggressive have been doves. This avian imagery has long been and strangely continues to be familiar to 'Our Political Correspondent' at Westminster. For him the doves are thought to be roosting in the area which is in fact a starlings' dormitory. When there is a leakage of supposedly confidential news he tells his readers that 'the dove-cots have been fluttered in Whitehall'. The environs of Downing Street are forever a Columbarium in his eyes.

If there is a fluttering in the nests of hawks and falcons it can only be provoked by eagles whose adjective aquiline is usually applied to facial features. The Washington pressmen who hover round the Pentagon might employ accipitrine as a variant for their customary hawkish. A poet far removed from the corridors of military power brought it to my mind. Francis Thompson cried:

Oh for a will accipitrine to pursue.

The word fitted powerfully into the poetic style and taste of his time. Accipiter is Latin for a hawk. He was a Latinist in his choice of language and so are many Americans who, on their way to home or office in the sky, say 'Operate the elevator' when we say 'Take the lift'. If they use eight syllables instead of three, why not prefer the lengthy and resonant accipitrine to the meagre hawkish?

Mention of Columbarium, the Latin for dove-cot, and the accipitrine types in the District of Columbia reminds me that a Columbiad is 'an epic of American life'. That might make the hawks gnash their beaks, if beaks can be so treated when their owners are, to change the metaphor, 'blowing their tops'. How infuriating for them that Columbus shared so much of his name with the dove-cot and its cooing turtles. More about hawkish matters and terminology will be found in my later note on Glede.

Arrack

Derived from an Arabic word meaning 'Sweat juice'. After that sticky and nauseous thought comes the information that in Eastern countries arrack 'is any spirituous liquor of native manufacture'. To mention manufacture instead of distilling suggests a potent form of hooch, a word which Eric Partridge explains is 'Ex Alaska, hoochino, a very strong drink made by Alaskan natives'. The Alaskans had climatic justification. The Orientals had less need for central heating. The English brought the word arrack back from the East and applied it to a brew of punch.

'Boz' in his sketch of 'Vauxhall Gardens by Daylight' deplored 'the lack of magic and mystery caused by absence of illumination among the temples, saloons and cosmoramas'. He recorded rumours that in daytime under the trees 'studious men were constantly engaged in chemical experiments with the view of discovering how much water a bowl of negus could possibly bear'. Negus we may take to be the arrack which appears in a Vauxhall refreshments price-list of his time. Astonishingly it cost 'ten shillings per bowl'. (The catering trade was then displaying its Latin scholarship by the use of per instead of for, a practice which long continued in the 'tea per pot per person' in the humbler bills of fare.) Ten shillings was then a vast sum; a working-class family could be housed, fed and clothed on twenty shillings a week. Bob Cratchit managed on fifteen and had a goose for Christmas. Unless the arrack bowl was enormous its contents should have been potent. 'Boz' did not report any discovery of the whispered watering of the negus before the night's gaieties began.

Vauxhall was not for the needy. 'Boz' was charged a shilling as entrance money even in dismal daylight. The patrons of the Gardens paid little for the spirituous and lavishly for the vinous uplifters. Gin, rum and whisky were sixpence a glass which was far above public-house prices. Spirits, now so extortionately taxed, were at Vauxhall common stuff for common folk who would want a fair-sized tot for their tanner and not the miserable nips of today. Brandy, at a shilling, was for less common patrons.

Wines were strangely expensive. The list includes 'Bucellas', a white Portuguese at five shillings. 'Champagne, Moetts' (there were two t's then in that historic name) was priced at twelve shillings a bottle and 'Old Hock, Iced' at ten. If those charges are related to the general cost of living the Vauxhall night out was only for the affluent or the fortunate poor who had had a lucky break. Only a man already elevated beyond caring would put down half a sovereign for a bowl of possibly enfeebled arrack.

Author and Authority

An article in *Punch* on the specialists whom journalists are often glad to quote provided the Fleet Street grading of these consultants. They move up the ladder from a mere expert to an authority and then to a leading authority. This was discussed in a handsomely produced magazine issued by an historic house of vintners. The author of it said that by a gossip columnist he would probably be described and cited as 'Wineman Berry'. It was not a description which he welcomed, but presumably the publicity and the attribution of authority and leadership in that rank were acceptable. What he did not like was the journalistic habit of dropping the ifs and buts in the brief and brisk reporting of supposedly authoritarian statements. Will this be a wonderful year for Bordeaux? The 'wineman' is optimistic with qualifications. But it is assumed that readers of newspapers, while glad to hear the voice of authority, have no appetite for the hypothetical. Give them the quick and confident 'quote'.

Diffident authority is unpopular. The interrogating gossip man is not looking for a wineman's delicately balanced opinion. The duty of an expert is first to be certain and then short and sharp in saying so. If there is a dearth of headline news the small stuff will have to serve as matter for expertise. 'The day will surely come,' continued the wineman's editorial, 'when a big story breaks about hot-water bottles and Fleet Street will be frantically searching for the leading authority in this field.' So, when that pundit has been found and duly pestered on the telephone we shall be favoured with the views of Ace Bottleman Biggs. Out with the bedside, or rather the in-the-bed, story. This can be warmed up by adding the thermal choice of the latest with-it girl, perfectly photographed cuddling her comforter. Authority has spoken.

The word author originally meant one who adds or increases. The most correctly named in this kind is therefore the auctioneer who by persuasive 'gab' in the market-place or by the reticent, almost silent, pressure of his authority in the august sale-room sets prices soaring. There, in a Bond Street setting, the bidders are no less tacit. What a bank balance must be behind the assenting nod which signals another hundred pounds by a motion of the head or thousands in the new valuation of Old Masters. Win or lose, the supreme Noddies never show emotion. An auction at the highest level does not evoke a smile, much less a cheer. The purchaser is mutely wondering to what extent he can be an author in the old sense by adding to the price when he sells what he has so expensively bought.

The author early became the maker with God at the summit, as 'the Author and Creator of all things'. He then dwindled to be the mere writer of books which, if new, are hard to sell and do little to increase an income. But the standard works on any subject retain the decisive authority which they have long held. By Shakespeare's time the bookish author was so called by him, the greatest in this class. Berowne in *Love's Labour's Lost* thought that a woman's face was more potent than any string of words:

> Now where is any author in the world
> Teaches such beauty as a woman's eyes?

The same speaker knew also of authority in the sense of exemplary knowledge and took the poor view of it natural to one who was a natural poet and sneered at by the learned and labouring University men.

> What have continual plodders ever won
> Save base authority from others' books?

But Shakespeare was aware that elsewhere there is need of the stored knowledge that would be a bore in the theatre.

Quillman Shakespeare, as he might have been called if there had been gossip journalism in his time, contributed to the play of *Pericles* whose last three acts include, along with some superb poetry signed by its splendour, the interesting character of the doctor Cerimon. This was written after Dr John Hall, a notable Warwickshire medico, had become his son-in-law and neighbour. It is emphasised that Cerimon has diligently applied himself to the required reading. Says he:

> 'Tis known I ever
> Have studied physic, through which secret art,
> By turning o'er authorities I have,
> Together with my practice, made familiar
> To me and to my aid, the blest infusions
> Which dwell in vegetives, in metals, stones.

Thus instructed Dr Hall built up his practice in another sense and became the chief consultant of the local squires and titled gentry, an expert, authority and leading authority. He had been the continual plodder; he had won status, reward and the hand of Susanna Shakespeare who was remembered on her tombstone as virtuously 'wise to salvation' and as charmingly 'witty beyond her sex'. Dr Hall was an author of the quillman kind, writing his case books in Latin; he was also the author of an approved and profitable career, while his father-in-law was the author of his steadily increasing property in land around his home.

Azyme

Azyme, meaning 'a Jewish cake of unleavened bread' and also the Passover day itself, follows the note on Authority for a strange reason. I had been wondering about the Authorised Version of the Bible which was completed in 1615. The Dedication, in which the fulsome could not be more finely worded, salutes 'The most high and mighty Prince James' as one whose very name is 'precious to his loyal and religious people'. Accordingly the translators 'bless you in their hearts as that Sanctified Person who, under God, is the immediate Author of their true happiness'. They offer their labours 'to Your Majesty, not only as our King and Sovereign but as the principal Mover and Author of the work'. They expect, as do all writers on any subject, 'the censures of ill-meaning and discontented persons' but hope that the royal 'allowance and acceptance shall more honour and encourage us than the calumniations and hard interpretations of other men shall dismay us'.

To call King James sanctified was carrying adulation rather far. To add that he was a most tender and loving nursing father of God's word was partially true. Had he not originated the translator's devoted toil the English language would have lacked the greatest piece of prose in its possession. That Bible did not carry the name of 'Authorised Version'. This, the Oxford English Dictionary tells us, was 'a popular appellation'.

Back to azyme. In their preface called 'The Translators to the Reader' we are told that 'we have avoided the scrupulosity of the Puritans who leave the old Ecclesiastical words and betake them to others, as when they put "washing" for "baptism" and "congregation" instead of "church": also on the other side we have shunned the obscurity of the Papists in their "azymes", "tunik", "rational", "holocausts", "prepuce", "pasche" and a number of such like'. These were said 'to darken the sense' and defeat understanding. 'We desire that the Scripture may speak like itself, as in the language of Canaan, that it may be understood even of the very vulgar.' Prepuce, for foreskin, might be a puzzle, but why were the Translators so reluctant to admit rational and call a tunic a tunic? By 1600 rational was accepted as meaning 'having sound judgment, sensible', but evidently it was little known to the vulgar, and quite beyond the comprehension of the very vulgar for whom the Anglican Authorities were so zealously caring, while making sure that the uncircumcised were made aware of what Christianity allowed them to retain.

B

Babble-wren

The wren has always had what is called 'a good press'. Shakespeare, with his particularly sharp eye for the miniscule, delighted in his 'tiny quill'. In his plays there are nine mentions of the wren compared with ten for the far more celebrated nightingale, the constant pet of the poets. The two are companions in Ralph Hodgson's glorious 'Song of Honour':

> The nightingale and babble-wren
> Were in the English greenwood then.

The babble-wren? Here is a name unknown to the ornithologists and lexicographers. Howard Saunders in his *Manual of British Birds*, a classic which includes a large number of occasional visitors, listed with the Common Wren, the Fire-crested, the Gold-crested, the Ruby-crowned, a rarity once wickedly shot near Loch Lomond, and the St Kilda, another rarity 'not sufficiently distinct to be worthy of specific rank'. After them come in the index the Willow Wren and Wood Wren. But they are not wrens; they are warblers, summer migrants who only arrive when the English greenwood is beginning to show its colours. Hodgson's babbler was a wandering voice. When he had the apocalyptic trance which evoked his poem—

> The babble-wren and nightingale
> Sang in the Abyssinian vale
> That season of the year.

Both the willow and the wood wren like to winter in Africa while our Jenny is not averse to wild Decembers at home. Either Hodgson invented the name of babble-wren, a charming fancy, or had heard it used by some countryman.

Portia, in her garden at Belmont, remarked that

> The nightingale, if she should sing by day,
> When every goose is cackling, would be thought
> No better a musician than the wren.

Like Juliet she was wrong about the sex. The Elizabethan bird-lovers were not aware that the songsters are a male voice choir.

The short and simple, native and Old English name of wren is a happy one for this popular midget, admired for its bravery as well as its looks. Lady

Macduff was paying it a possibly justified compliment when she said that it,

> The most diminutive of birds, will fight
> Her young ones in her nest, against the owl.

It is not too fanciful to suppose that Shakespeare had seen such a defensive action fought one evening on his own home-ground.

In the classical catalogue the wren is Troglodytes Parvulus; in the lexicon he is a dentirostral passerine, i.e. a sparrow-type 'having a tooth or notch on both sides of the mandible'. One cannot think of him as 'a spadger'. But Troglodyte, cave-dweller, he can be since he frequently chooses for his home a niche in a crannied wall or a hole in the ground of an ivy-covered bank. Hodgson's babble-wren must have been a warbler, one of the Sylvinae to the classifier. In any case the wren is given tribute for his music if he is associated with the Willow Wren whose name comes as musically to the ear at any time as does his song, with its plaintive dying fall, in proud-pied April or the flush of May. Hodgson's name suggests that a good place in which to hear that melody would be beside 'the stripling Thames at Bablock Hythe'.

Barbellate

I do not sing to myself 'How beautiful they are, the hairy ones' when I see on the television screen a parade of young protest marchers whose capillary fashions are now deemed essential to the holders of advanced views. There is an irony here. While the political opinions of the demonstrators are radical or revolutionary their decision to be hirsute is Tory and traditional. Conservatives cannot censure the cultivation of plentiful face-fungus as a nastiness of our time. When the razor had long been invented the dandies as well as the militant men let their tresses flow down the neck either in natural growth or elegant perruque. Chins and cheeks had also their ample foliage and so earned the English form of the Latin adjective barbellate. That word brings to mind the angler's barbel so called because 'filaments' hang down from the mouth of this fresh-water fish. He is not a handsome fellow, but how many fishes are? Lithe and graceful in action they may be, but the piscine profile rarely looks what is called 'a picture'. But down the centuries the human male who could have shaved favoured the filaments of barbellation.

When shaving was laborious and the instruments crude there was an obvious saving of effort in letting the filaments luxuriate. It is curious that the ancient Romans who lacked the aesthetic sensibility of the Greeks and were proud of their manly and martial vigour chose, at least among the upper class of Tiber-siders, to be clean-shaven. Yet their razors cannot have approached the keenness eloquently advertised in the case of modern safety blades. So they have left us the word tonsorial as well as the adjective barbellate. The Greeks have given us the language used in the craft of trichology, the 'haute couture' of hair which recently soared very high indeed when a woman's crowning glory once more became her wig.

The Victorian dandy sported a good whisker. The household article of that name was a light brush used to flick away dust or flies. But there was nothing flimsy about the bushy sprouting on the face. It spread and it drooped. A famous stage character gave to one of its forms the name of Dundreary. For the bristly types there was the Latin adjective setaceous. In the late Victorian drawing-rooms where George du Maurier's gentry joined the ladies there was plenty of hair to be seen. For Tennyson there could be a look of learning in the foliage on the cheek. He wrote of

> Slight Sir Robert with his watery smile
> And educated whisker.

Not only the bourgeois chose to be shrubby about the chaps and gills. The leaders of free and fearless thought, no watery smilers, Karl Marx and H. M. Hyndman on the Socialist platform and Ibsen and Shaw in the theatre, had forests on the cheeks. We talk now of sideburns, a word hard to explain. Whiskers are certainly side-line ornaments but they do not blaze unless the owner is exceptionally rufous. The youthful G. B. S. thus qualified for the sideburn label.

Then came an interval. Setacity went out of fashion. There was recourse to the neglected razor. At the turn of the last century, there came a turn of the trend, a rape of the lock and an ebbing of the hairy tide. When I was an undergraduate there was not a beard or a whisker to be seen among my coevals and very few among the elders at High Table.

> 'Tis merry in hall,
> When beards wag all,

sang Mr Justice Silence over the pippins and caraways when he was a fellow-guest with Falstaff in Gloucestershire. Thus suggests a tiresome kind of senile titter at High Tables but now the young beardies can wag away, one hopes merrily, over their dinner-time sessions.

When the close clip and the clean shave became general the errand-boys liked to shout 'There's 'air' at the sight of a superfluous tress. Later came the derisive cry of 'Beaver' when a beard was seen. Now such mockery is silent because the targets are too many. No cry of 'Goldilocks' is heard when the yellowish foliage once described as filemot (feuille morte) is on view. The hairies have returned to power, confident of acceptance, and even proud of the usually scruffy appendage to their jaws. Their lady-friends are complacently permissive. Is a kiss more coveted if the lover's lips are setaceous?

If men are to be 'valanced', to use Hamlet's word, I would prefer the curtains, if they must be present, to be under control. The elegant courtiers at the Elizabethan palaces took their beards to the sign of the pole for trimming and combing. They knew that barbellation requires barbering and that even the most educated whisker needs its discipline.

Bassinet

The bassinet has a floral life as 'a species of ranunculus or geranium.' Its domestic function, in or outside the home, is that of a baby's perambulator. Perhaps I should say 'was'; I think the name is not much in use now. The pram has prevailed.

I was set thinking of this by an advertisement which I noticed in a most informative reprint of the 1861 Christmas number of 'The Queen'. The nation was in general mourning for the recent death of the Prince Consort and the Victorian costumiers (no 'rag trade' then) were offering blacks in plenty to the ladies who were certainly well wrapped up. Black petticoats were offered in Quilted Alpaca, Quilted Llama Wool, Quilted Lustre, Quilted Glacé and Eiderdown in black Alpaca. For the equestriennes there were 'Riding Trousers in Chamois leather with black feet' for wearing under the voluminous skirt.

There were the new arrivals to remember. For them one shop announced its Babies' Berceaunettes, another, less Parisian, its bassinets. There was no mention of the perambulator. Berceau is French for a cradle and berceuse for a rocking-chair. Barcelonette was a word for a swing-cot. The Anglicised bassinet had first been mentioned in English homes in 1854. It was doubtless regarded as more refined and better suited to readers of 'The Queen' than the perambulator which acquired its meaning of a baby carriage in the same year. Hitherto that word had been used for a pedometer used by walkers for measuring the distance covered. The now abbreviated pram was not used, according to Oxford, until 1884. The berceaunette or bassinet had quite a long outing in the parks and gardens where the nannies gathered and gossiped. Were their infantile inmates protected from the December weather by a coverlet of Black Quilted Eiderdown? The display of grief was universal and the bassinet might be expected to participate in the loyal and lugubrious trend.

Blate

The Scot has acquired the adjective canny. He is thought to have his feet on the ground, his shrewd head on his broad shoulders and his eye sensibly directed to the main chance, without neglect of honest dealing. Yet, as a word-maker (once a makar to him) he has shown an astonishing delight and fertility in the naming of fools. Caledonia, it seems, has been a constant nurse of the moronic child. This was pointed out in an address on the Scottish character given to the Greenock Philosophical Society by James Bridie of whose wisdom more will be found in the note on navel.

He mentioned the loon who was blate. By starting with that he began gently on the lower slopes of crudeness and crassness. Blate first meant pale, nervous and inarticulate; then it was applied to stupidity. With that suggestion it has been accepted in English dictionaries. It is not a damning word. The English equivalent might be dim, a word once common in University slang for a dull, agreeable fellow with nothing much to say. Recently he has been less politely called a drip.

Robert Burns wrote of the time when he was 'beardless, young, and blate'. He remained unbarbellated and he lacked the years in which to grow old. But, if ever he was shy in feminine company or speechless among the drouthy males in tavern company, he soon grew out of that. He may in his cups have passed from blateness to the talking of blathers or blethers and been thought a blatherskite. The Scots have fully appreciated the explosive and blasting force of a 'bl' at the beginning of a word. But Burns would not have qualified for the remarkable assortment of nouns and adjectives with which his countrymen thumped the supposedly thick heads of the dense. The fools have been called thowless, gowking gomerils, three bludgeoning words for those who cannot think and gaze stupidly about. If the idiot was aggressively noisy instead of quietly blate he was a routing sump or a wulliewalloch. If a woman of that species was a wanton as well as a wallocher she was a foutering taupie. The broader the Scots language the more was the relish in the description of the clot.

The quick-witted were gleg and the smart lad was a glibbans, but one hears and reads much less of them. If the Scots have deemed themselves to be superior persons, with which vanity they have been charged, they have modestly concealed the fact in their vernacular, which has richly labelled those worse than blate as daft, donnart and doited.

Britzka

The horse-drawn carriage pulled into English usage a number of impressive foreign names. The Victorians were not content with their own light, four-wheeled Victoria. They had inherited from the Georgians the French barouche and cabriolet and the German landau. They also favoured the Polish Britzka 'an open carriage with a calash top and space for reclining'. I have just read of one of these in which a father and mother rode with their small boy 'bodkin'. That was the name given to 'a person wedged in between two others when there is room for two only'. It must be a shortening of the diminutive noun bodikin, a little fellow. A big bodkin would be a contradictory term and an unpopular passenger. How long did the name survive? Two-seater motor-cars are frequently overloaded with a third party squeezed in. But I have never heard talk of a bodkin in our midst.

The Britzka suggests by its sound a brisk and skittish conveyance very different from the august barouche and landau. The calash or calèche was a light carriage with a hood and then was a name for the hood itself. From the trap it was transferred to the feminine wardrobe. On wet days if a woman lacked one kind of calash for transport she walked with another on her head and shoulders for shelter. The Russian droshky did not become a regular carriage-title in Britain, perhaps because the name suggests to us a shabby and bedraggled article, with a slightly drunken driver. It was used in slang for a cab.

One cannot imagine a Victorian grandee asking a flunkey if his droshky was at the door. Britzka would be more U, as we say now. Vehicular snobbery does not dwindle. In our motor-car vocabulary we work our way up through the animal and avian worlds from the snipe to the raptors. Is there a Gazelle for the Jaguar to overtake on the road without, one hopes, lethal results? The ambitious traveller also works his way to the legal summit and becomes a Master of the Rolls.

Brothel

There was a time when a normal reader or play-goer was revolted by the poxy humours of Shakespeare's brothel scenes in *Measure for Measure* and *Pericles*. Now the scope of theme and licence of speech in all kinds of writing have reduced their attraction to the smut-seeking adolescent. It has been surmised that Shakespeare wrote of the stews with personal experience and painful results. This is a rash assumption. He wrote of many things and places without personal knowledge or contact. He had his eyes and his ears at work amid the traffic of the town. He lodged for a while amid the South Bank's commerce in debauchery. The local women named after their worshipful ground-landlord as 'the Bishop of Winchester's geese' were in full gaggle and cackle close to the Globe Theatre. Bawds and pandars were his neighbours. That does not prove that he was a customer. Nor is his acquaintance with the results of venereal disease evidence of a personal affliction.

He does not use the word brothel as often as might be expected, twice in *King Lear* and only once in four other plays. It is a curious word, unconnected with broth and derived from an Old English root meaning broken. The brothel was a broken man, a wreck, before it was his house of call. The bawd began as a bold and reckless person. The name was later limited to a single and vicious occupation. If the Elizabethan bawd prospered he or she took his chance of being carted and flogged through the streets as well as of imprisonment in the Bridewell (ironic title) across the river from the Southwark shore. Boldness was required.

The vocabulary of vice is curious. Brothel began as a man. So did harlot. To Chaucer he could be a commendable type. His 'Somonour' was 'a gentil harlot and a kynde', 'a bettre felaw sholde men noght finde'. The Somonour's virtue was not of an austere kind. He would lend his concubine for a year to 'a good felawe' for a quart of wine. This suggests the generosity of a poor bargainer but also indicates that the masculine harlot was far from being a homosexual.

Concubine is biblical and legal. One might hear it now in jest. Strumpet is a mystery evading capture by the lexicographers. Whatever its origin, it is too light and playful a word to imply much censure. The Old English whore makes the right sound for a damning dismissal with hell-fire in the background. The Victorians shunned it and it remained unusable in some strict printing houses during the first quarter of this century. One newspaper refused to mention in its theatrical news a production of John Ford's play *'Tis Pity She's a Whore*. There would have been no objection to strumpet. The Elizabethan range of slang names for 'the daughters of the game' as Troilus called them was enormous. Ben Jonson was not thinking of a masseuse when he brought a fricatrice into his dialogue. Nor was Shakespeare considering a drab when he mentioned a kicky-wicky. That was an affectionate name for a wife. It brings us back from the city stews to the suburbs of respectability.

Bum

The word is both less polite and more effective than the usual bottom. Not long ago it was considered too vulgar to appear in respectable books and papers. I was reminded of this by a note in Janet Adam Smith's excellent edition of Robert Louis Stevenson's Collected Poems. The third set of verses in the section of 'Underwoods' written in Scots begins:

> When aince Aprile has fairly come,
> An' birds may bigg in winter's lum,
> An' pleisure's spreid for a' and some
>> O' whatna state,
> Love, wi' her auld recruitin' drum,
>> Than taks the gate.

Miss Adam Smith notes that 'the manuscript notebook of Stevenson's' headed 'Pieces in Lallans' gives a variant and rejected version of the second and third lines:

> An' winter turned his icy bum
> Wi' pleasand days for a' and some.

This must have been put aside as too coarse for late Victorian taste. So, for the sake of rhyme, the lum (chimney) replaced the vernacular for bottom.

But 'winter's icy bum' strikes the right chill in a resounding and memorable way. Stevenson felt the cold bitterly and his poems are frore with the Edinburgh winters of his childhood and youth. His widow wrote that 'he was unfortunate in having to endure in infancy the climate of Edinburgh with its cold mists and penetrating east winds', but Sir Compton Mackenzie in his admirable contribution to the International Profiles Series maintained, with long personal experience of the Scottish capital, that 'Stevenson himself must bear the chief blame

34

for the vulgar belief that the sun rarely shines in Edinburgh. The winters of his childhood may have coincided with a particularly bad run of winters. To-day Edinburgh has more sunshine, particularly in winter, than any other large city in Great Britain.'

None the less R.L.S. remembered the iciness of winter's protuberant rear when he was writing in Scots. His mention of the withdrawal of winter's buttocks is linked with the arrival of April when he could escape, 'couthy and bien', into

> A bonny bit
> Atween the muckle Pentland's knees.

Until that comes the winter's posterior is reasonably thought of as gelid in Scotland's capital. I have attended Burns Night celebrations in that noble and hospitable city in January's bottom end. I encountered what Stevenson described as

> Nirly, nippin', Eas'lan' breeze
> Norlan' snaw and haar o' seas.

Sir Compton has been there more often and far longer than I have. I would not dispute his meteorological assessment of the solar radiation. His tribute to the Midlothian climate and Stevenson's intended use of the word bum remind me of the poem by Raymond Asquith (or to him attributed) which began:

> The sun like a bishop's bottom,
> Rosy and round and hot.

The climate so shiversome and possibly so damaging to Stevenson's boyhood has kindly cast a blaze on Sir Compton's window-panes. At any rate Stevenson was often lyrical about April. When winter's bum is protruding can spring be far behind?

Bumptious

Oxford is somewhat sniffy about this adjective. 'Colloquial and undignified' is the verdict. If so its use is not, I suppose, to be encouraged or even allowed by instructors in correct English. Its origin is obscure. Presumably it comes from that odd meaning of the noun bump which has nothing to do with a knock or a jolt. I read that a bump is 'one of those prominences of the cranium associated by phrenologists with special faculties or propensities'. Hence the man who knows his way about has 'the bump of locality'. The cranial protuberance may be the sign of wisdom but it has also been regarded as the excrescence of vanity and a lump on a swollen head.

The rustic bumpkin may be lumpish. So Goldsmith thought when he created his oafish Tony Lumpkin. I resent the banishment of bumptious from the confines of respectable writing. It so well describes the attitude of those ingenious persons who think they have a bump of remarkable perception when a play or a part of Shakespeare's is to be reinterpreted according to their new and revolutionary ideas. As a play-goer I have had to endure that affliction too often. Bumptious is exactly the adjective for them since it suggests the stupidity of the bumpkin as well as the conceit of the cranially protuberant type. It may be undignified but it comes down with a bump where such a rap is properly required.

C

Camelopard and Others

The camelopard is an 'African ruminant quadruped with long neck, long legs and a spotted skin', more commonly known as the giraffe. (Whenever I read of ruminant animals I think of them as ruminating pensively and that may sometimes be the mood of an introverted camelopard.) The name is a verbal mating of the camel because of his shape and the leopard because of his markings.

I have been reminded by a student of nomenclature as well as zoology that a new hybrid has appeared requiring a new name. The address of this arrival is romantically far-western, Cedar Point Amusement Park, Safari Island, Sandusky, Oregon. There a lioness and a tiger co-operated in the production of three cubs with black stripes on a tan coat. They are to winter in the Caribbean Gardens at Naples, Florida. Meanwhile the father, however good a husband, is suspected of disliking his progeny and has been parted from them. There is a question as to their label. Are they Tigons or Ligers? If the principle of male ascendancy be accepted they must be Tigons. At the time of writing they were only eight inches long and weighed less than a pound. May they enlarge and survive and not only to amuse, as tigons, tigons burning bright, the pleasure-seekers on the two extremes of the American continent.

Another remarkable hybrid and comrade in nomenclature of the camelopard and the tigon is the chameleon, a protean reptile able to change his colour as quickly as the nimble politician, 'promise-crammed'. So Hamlet thought of this versatile snake which, in his opinion, was satisfied with a diet of oxygen. The Greek origin of his name was a blending of the lion and the earth on which he crawled. If the lion has its pride in the ordinary sense there may be some affront here. Is the king of beasts to be verbally married to a creepy-crawly?

Carphology

By origin, a clutching at straws, a habit or nervous tic, known to the renowned Greek doctor who practised in Rome as Claudius Galenus in the second century B.C. He provided this name for the ailment from which Falstaff suffered at the end. Carphology is 'the movements of delirious persons, as of searching for imaginary objects, or picking the bedclothes'. Reading of this affliction I at once remembered Mistress Quickly's superbly compassionate and detailed description of Sir John's death. 'After I saw him fumble with his sheets and play with flowers and smile upon his fingers I knew there was but one way; for his nose was as sharp as a pen and a' babbled of green fields.'

Babbled is a famous and much accepted emendation of the Folio's 'table of green fields' which seems meaningless. If babbled is correct (it is a verb which Shakespeare frequently used), I like the suggestion made to me by W. Bridges-Adams, a great director of Shakespeare's plays, that the old man was muttering of 'green sleeves' since 'My Lady Green Sleeves' with its sweet, sad air was the most popular song of the period. Perhaps, but there is a persuasive fancy in the idea of that tavern-haunting and very urban rake suddenly remembering the meadows of childhood or the London fields which at that time were near enough to Eastcheap. Bernard Shaw maintained that he was alluding to green frieze, the coarse cloth of which coverlets were made. The bedspread could have been green. But he was fumbling with his sheets not his blankets. The green fields fit in with the playing with flowers.

The comment on this point has been extensive. Whatever was the 'table' or the babble, a most poignant detail is the fidgeting with fingers turning cold and the clutching at imaginary things, perhaps Doll Tearsheet's hand, which the definition of carphology includes.

Carphology caused me to look into the career of Galen and so also of Hippocrates, Galen's senior by nearly three hundred years in the practice and teaching of medicine. Thus I learned that the originator of the famous oath of a doctor's dedication lived to the age of one hundred and three. The physician had efficiently healed himself, whatever maladies he had met and defeated during his work in many parts of Greece. One wonders who was Falstaff's doctor and what he thought of his patient and his chance of survival.

Carwitchet

This curious word appeared at the head of a theatrical review in the *Spectator* written by its recent critic, Hilary Spurling. Her subject was a revival of Ben Jonson's *Bartholomew Fair* with its panorama of London life in all its humours and chicanery. Those of her readers who did not know it probably found no explanation in their dictionaries. That it was not carried to America by any Pilgrim Father is shown by its absence from my gigantic Random House lexicon. I tracked it down at last in the glossary attached to the 'Everyman' volumes of Jonson's plays. It means 'a quip or pun', for which the Jonsonian alternatives were quib or quiblin. I prefer his carwitchet but the origin of that oddity is obscure. To me it first suggested the transport of a coven of Shakespeare's 'weird sisters', an outfit of broom-sticks.

Cheeky

Why cheek, defined as 'the part of the face below the eye' became a Victorian colloquial term for insolence, is a mystery. Perhaps the much older use of barefaced to mean audacious suggests an explanation. Our words for rudeness are a puzzling company. Insolence has had a curious change of usage. By derivation it means (and did once describe) unusual or unaccustomed behaviour. The switch from the strange to the insulting had come in Elizabethan English. Why did a word meaning rare become a word meaning rude? Politeness is not as common as churlishness. There is a remarkable optimism in the old assumption that the unaccustomed is the unmannerly.

A similar change has happened with impertinence. This originally meant irrelevance and can still do so. A precisian can tell a fellow-member of a committee that his proposal is impertinent without intending to accuse him of being cheeky. He is merely suggesting, in perhaps too pedantic a manner, that his colleague is deviating from the essential point. But, if that is the intention, there could be indignant misunderstanding.

Impudence provides another example of altered

meaning. Properly it implies lack of pudency or chastity. Shakespeare's Posthumus in *Cymbeline* attributed to Imogen 'a rosy pudency' before he was so easily fooled into believing that she was a wanton 'daughter of the game'. Now impudent has lost all its sexual pertinence. To apply that adjective is to signify cheek not lechery.

Pert is another word that has gone to the bad. Its original meaning was skilful, quick and nimble of limbs as well as wit. Milton's 'pert Fairies and the dapper Elves' who 'trip on the Tawny Sands and Shelves' were not being saucy. To speak now of a pert boy is to suggest an impudent lad, a 'smart Alec'. (Why the Alexanders have been regarded as typically smart or brash is another of the rudeness mysteries.) To the cheek as the seat of impudence we have added the lip. Yet lips can be reverently as well as offensively employed.

Chrysoprase

I have in the past regretted the narrow and spare vocabulary of some recent poets. T. S. Eliot frankly admitted that he put the muse 'on a lean diet' and he set a fashion in verbal austerity. Therefore I was grateful to discover in an anthology of bad verse, *The Stuffed Owl*, collected and annotated by D. B. Wyndham Lewis, the work of Thomas Holley Chivers (fl. 1840) who in rapture turned the sparkle of jewels into jewels of speech. In praise of a well-regarded Miss Rosalie Lee he paraded a striking mixture of fruit, flowers and precious stones:

> Many mellow Cydonian suckets,
>   Sweet apples, anthosmial, divine,
> From the ruby-rimmed beryline buckets,
>   Star-gemmed, lily-shaped, hyaline:

> Like the sweet golden goblet found growing
>   On the wild emerald cucumber-tree,
> Rich, brilliant, like chrysoprase glowing,
>   Was my beautiful Rosalie Lee.

He was slightly repeating himself since chrysoprase
is a variety of beryl and so of a greenish lustre. I find
his colour-scheme confusing. The ruby-rimmed and
beryline buckets must be the apple-blossom, which
is usually more pink than ruby-red. But at the end of
the verse the taking features of Miss Lee have added
to a golden glow the appearance of chrysoprase to
which the dictionary allots a green colouring. Could
the lady admired by T. H. Chivers really have been
so tinted? He does not indicate that she was a vic-
time of nausea or apt to change her complexion in
those moments of fright which impose a hyaline or
glassy look. The 'mellow Cydonian suckets' bring the
quince into the picture. But one must not cavil.
High regard is due to a poet who was determined to
save the muse from word-starvation. And who can
grudge applause for the readiness to rhyme bucket
and sucket in praise of feminine beauty and in a
song of love abounding?

Cleek, Spoon and Others

Golf has fashioned its own 'speak' and a fine one.
The language of the greens beside the blue has more
than its own fascination for the addicts. It makes
a pleasant noise for any ear. The very sound of a
fairway could not be more beckoning. It is an invitation to be there. To those who, like myself, once
muddled their way happily over Gullane hill the
sight of the whole of the south of Scotland from the
hills of the Neuk across the Firth to the Lammer-
muirs on the southern verge was a glory in itself and

must have been heaven indeed to those who never jarred their hands or dashed their hopes with a foozle or a vagrant shot. And what a melody of neighbouring link-names was in the air around from the smiling welcome of Kilspindie to the trumpet-call of Tantallon! The championship courses put music in the air: St Andrews, Muirfield, Carnoustie, Hoylake, Birkdale. Like Kipling's English flowers 'almost singing themselves they run'.

For the senile and chair-bound there is still a genuine sense of holiday and a sniff of the salt as we watch the masters on our television sets with colour, and preferably with Henry Longhurst, as affable as expert, acting as our guide to the terrain beside the sands and the surf where the masters are achieving their birdies and eagles. To hear those avian names for masterly achievements is to listen to the larks soaring over Muirfield in May or think of a kestrel overhead as it often is at London's Mid-Surrey. Golfers, be they tigers or rabbits, have remembered their natural history when they invent their lingo.

The most gifted of writers about golf in his time and a delightful essayist on many a theme, Bernard Darwin, called one of his pieces 'The Sound of Golf'. In the days of wooden clubs, he said, 'old Tom Morris used to speak of the music of a shaft, meaning the spring or whip in it, a poetical thought.' But Darwin accepted the 'swish' of the new steel. In its own metallic way it was adding to the agreeable noises of the game. He continued, 'When I first bought a particularly engaging little spoon, its music seemed infinitely exciting and romantic.' We now miss, and some of us mourn, the old vocabulary.

Among the vanished names that symbol of steadiness, Colonel Bogey, has been replaced by the more exacting and less picturesque 'par'. There are no spoons now. Arithmetic has coldly supplanted the descriptive names of cordial affection. When one of the supreme eagle-hunters knows that to go far is less important than to go straight, since the hazards of a pull or a slice may be ruinous to his score-card, the commentator tells us that he has chosen a number three wood. (The wood of course applies only to the club-head.) Yet, oddly and happily, there is still mention of the ancient driver as well as of a number one wood.

The other names of the clubs, a strange, endearing company, have gone. Most young players have never heard them. The spoon was also a baff. Since the dictionary's definition of a baff is a 'blow with anything soft, a slap with the palm of the hand' a baffy is hardly an accurate name for a number three wood when Jack Nicklaus, that golden tiger of the game, takes it in his powerful claw. The word cleek began as a verb meaning to grasp firmly in the hand. It is now, as a noun, a number one iron. It is odd that the irons have never become the steels.

One of Bernard Darwin's memorable essays was a paean in praise of J. H. Taylor's use of that weapon, most notably when the Open Championship was being played at Hoylake. The wind and rain were terrific. J. H. chose a cleek for his second shot, glued himself to the sodden, slippery turf and sent his ball whizzing in the very teeth of the storm to the heart of the green. 'There never was such a cleek shot; there never will be such another as the world stands.' So Cleek is a name immortalised for me by 'Bernardo' who wrote even better than he played. To hell with the number one iron!

So down the scale of potency we go. The mashie was not a club for violence. It yielded a stroke which might be as mild as its name. There is a dictionary verb to mash which curiously meant both to make affectionate approaches to a lady (so, incidentally, did spoon) and to break stones. One did indeed make approaches to the green with a mashie and its

44

chip-shot. But one was not fragmenting granite. The name lingers gently and suavely in the mind.

Next came the niblick, a word whose origin defies the lexicographers. Sometimes rather tamely called a lofter, it was used for extrication from a bunker or deep, tenacious grass. In this case we are spared more arithmetic. The niblick has been replaced by the sand-wedge, which is now employed with such fiendish efficiency by the champions that instead of just seeking to escape somehow and somewhere from the caverns round the green they expect to be close to the hole, whatever their position in the sand.

The old niblick had ferocity in its title. Who was it who said of what steep-faced bunker that the man who designed it should have been buried with a niblick driven through his heart? That damnation would have lost half the impetus if sand-wedge had been mentioned instead of the properly grim, harsh-sounding niblick. Fortunately a putter is still just that and not a number ten iron. So at the extremes the happy nomination remains while numeration dulls the intervening range of peaceful weapons. The tranquillity of golf must be thankfully remembered at a time when several sports need constant police protection. International contests on the links do not lead to rage and riot. Referees are not bottle-pelted. The spectators are not seeking trouble or smashing up trains. Among the performers tempers may occasionally be lost by a duffer but the object of rage and objurgations is a bad lie or a hellish bunker and not one's opponent. Club is an aggressive word but it is not used for clobbering. Calm is the mood and soothing is the melody of golfing names and places.

Climatologically

The headquarters of the sky-reading prophets are sensibly and briefly described as the British Weather Centre, but the language used there is not so terse. 'Climatologically speaking' were the opening words of a recent statement. The forecaster who chose this verbal gambit could have added that he was speaking as a representative of meteorological epistemology.

The elements of his subject have short and simple names, sun and moon, sky and shower, wind and water. But they do not suffice when science starts to consider and explain their output. I anticipate a time when, climatologically speaking, these old friends of the lyric and song writers, either of the poetical or the brashly 'pop', yield to a syndrome of Atlantic depressions which are confronting an anti-cyclonic complex. There will be in attendance some of those isobars which to some listeners more urgently suggest a slab of 'choc-ice' in the cinema than equality of barometric pressure. Fortunately many of the expounders realise that they are addressing large numbers of people who only want to know about the prudent wearing of a mackintosh or carrying of an umbrella.

Our weather language is a fascinating mixture. The umbrella should be a sun-shade but experience has made it the 'weather-fending' gamp. The adjective is Shakespearian and the noun Dickensian. Hey, ho, the wind and the rain! *King Lear*, climatologically speaking, added richly to the vocabulary of downpour. There are torrents wherever we turn in the weather dictionary. The mackintosh comes from the Scottish Highlands where the Atlantic depressions linger round the peaks. If we say that we are under the weather we have no blue skies in mind. The word weather itself began its life meaning a gale. As a verb it implies storms to be endured. I remember a boyhood song which announced:

> Whatever the weather
> We'll weather it together
> When Lusitania Lucy's mine.

Could a declaration of steadfast love have been more ominous?

Crats

This morning I encountered Eurocrats in my morning paper and meritocrats in the evening. The former was puzzling. Who were bossing the continent from Portugal to the borders of Siberia? One answer would be the top échelon (journalists are now very fond of an échelon), of the technologists who have become technocrats. They are the autocrats, faceless and formidable, unelected and uncontrolled. They have discoverable addresses, I suppose, in universities and research stations. They prevail in those corridors of power which have become a cliché, but are a fact. The technocrats silently scheme our entire way of life. The bureaucrats sign the orders; the democrat thinks that his parliament is sovereign. He is a pathetic survivor of a once promising faith, a poor dreamer, if he is allowed any sleep by the over-head roar of mammoth super-jets for which he never asked and has to pay. The technocrats are the cosmocrats and therefore must include the Eurocrats.

Those Eurocrats of whom I was reading are considerable potentates. They were explained as 'the officials who control the procedure of the Common Market'. When these remarks are printed the British may have been swept into their dominion.

My insufficiently instructed mind is baffled by the pros and cons of submission to these Big Bow-wows —or should they be called gnomes on the Zürich model—who will be Eurocratising in Brussels.

The crats abound and multiply. The meritocrats, already mentioned, are getting increasing attention. Obviously they are supposed to have influence according to their deserts. But who is the arbiter of merit, and how are the marks allotted? In a paragraph about the supposedly meritorious men, there was a most curious standard of grading. The writer was discussing parliamentary habits and costume. He described and also named the 'shaggy dogs' of Labour's left wing who wear roll-top sweaters at Westminster, spurning the collar-and-tie rule which is enforced in some restaurants and clubs. For some unexplained reason these woolly ones were called meritocrats and contrasted with the Tory barristers who come along from the Law Courts showing white linen at the neck above black coats and pin-stripe trousers. There is, it seems, complete absence of merit in the wearing of a clean collar.

The crat-folk grow more numerous and younger. Power is the operative word. We hear of Black Power which will give us autocrats and Student Power which will kick the gerontocrats out of the university senates and the headmasters' studies. I shall expect a campaign with the appropriate demos and protest marches organised by the pedocrats demanding pupil power down to infant school and kindergarten level. The one kind of crat most unlikely to appear, outside Roman Catholic countries, is the champion of theocracy with 'God the Invisible King'. That was surprisingly the title of a book by H. G. Wells when he was having a sudden seizure by a faith which he soon abandoned. Nor do I see much future for mesocracy, the rule of the middle-class. Small is their voting power, psephocracy, if we must keep the Greek vocabulary, as do the psephologists who tell us at election times what the figures mean. But out of the 'meso' class come many of the scientists, the men with the know-how, who make the arrangements which matter, the technocrats who are now the pan-crats.

Cuthbert

Those who have mastered Anglo-Saxon may know that a boy called Cuthbert should be a bright lad who becomes famous. Many have lived up to that label, but there are not so many of them now. During the 1914–18 war Cuthbert ceased to be a name and became an insult. The timid were dubbed Cuthberts. During that period bellicose ladies and men safely above the military age found great enjoyment in sending white feathers to those not in uniform and in denouncing the pacific or reluctant young men as Cuthberts, cowardy, cowardy Cuthberts. It was nonsensical. A Cuthbert could be as tough as a Leo or a Hector. But the idiocy lingered on and deterred parents choosing a name which has been rare since then.

If the anti-Cuthbert patriots had known any naval history they would have been aware that one of the most valiant and victorious of Britain's sailors in the Napoleonic Wars was Admiral Sir Cuthbert Collingwood, later Lord Collingwood, Nelson's brother-in-law, who took over the command of the Fleet when Horatio was killed at Trafalgar. Collingwood's career was a blaze of glory and his heroism renowned. To judge by his example, the name should be welcomed and honoured.

Other Christian names have been the victims of injustice. After the Wilde case in 1896 Oscar was exiled from christenings for some time. Despite the fact that Judas, not Iscariot, was a respected apostle, nobody would choose it for a son. If there were Judes they were obscure. Because the Grecian Sappho was later taken to be a depraved homosexual and corrupting influence (she was in fact a married woman with a daughter) not only her name but also that of her island, Lesbos, was taboo. The Oxford Dictionary of English Christian Names (1945) included a fine assortment of oddities, but did not mention Lesbia although Bernard Shaw had used it for an important and blameless character in his play *Getting Married* more than thirty years before that. In the prevailing climate of tolerant opinion one would expect some Lesbias to appear but they have not. Judas was not the only biblical name to suffer. With his too humble and hypocritical Heep, Dickens killed Uriah. This, though no beauty, had had some vogue, in Nonconformist families, which had also favoured Enoch. Why not? Enoch walked with God. But Arnold Bennett, christened Enoch Arnold Bennett, shook that off his sleeve and I cannot see a fervid devotee of racial integration now bestowing on his boy the name which the undaunted Mr Powell has refused to abandon.

One of the early Cuthberts was an Anglo-Saxon Saint of the seventh century. Seventy-two churches carry his name, which, if not one that charms the ear, has been delightfully smoothed by the Scots whose Kirkcudbright (Church of Cuthbert) in Galloway is spoken of with a dove-like murmur of Kirkcoobry. Travellers taking the western road to the Highlands should try a left turn after crossing the Border and visit the riverside town of that name. The air is soft, the atmosphere serene, the roads empty and the mixture of hills and inlets enchanting. Cuthbert's country honours the unjustly derided name.

There was a much earlier cruelty to Cuthbert.

Shortened to Cuddy, it was a donkey and also an asinine biped. In some Elizabethan plays Cuddy is a name given to the fool. But at least that discourtesy has died out. There may yet be a future for Cuthbert at the font, not least in and around Portsmouth and other home-grounds of naval families.

D

Demonetization

The careless reader of the first two syllables, reluctant to penetrate further into the mysterious verbal mess, might take it to signify collapse into demoniac fury. Its proper meaning, 'deprivation of standard monetary value', may indeed cause rage at what can simply be called a swindle. When I saw the word I took it to be a specimen of city editor's English in our time. But it turns out to be quite a veteran having been coined—I suppose that is the apposite word here—in 1853. No doubt it was used as a warning of horrors to come and to keep the bankers on their toes. The early Victorians surely were unflinching loyalists and sterling fellows, devoted to guarding the security of both kinds of sovereign. Apparently they knew of 'lesser breeds without the law' (Gresham's) and had this menacing word for its infringement.

Britain now walks a tight-rope striving to maintain its balance of payments. The undemonetized citizens of 1852 had their worries but they were not harassed by lack of exports although they diverted productive labour into personal service on a gigantic scale. I have seen it estimated that a fifth of the population of London was engaged in domestic service as butlers, cooks, coachmen, grooms, footmen, valets and feminine drudges of all menial kinds. Yet a society thus prodigal of its workers remained solvent. Its statesmen did not have to fly to Washington or crawl on their knees in Zürich to keep, or fail to keep, the demonetizing gnomes from further puncturing of the pound. The amount of service available to the Dickensian Veneerings was grotesque, but accepted. It is amusing to think of a Dombey or a Veneering confronted with Selective Employment Tax levied on every member of his staff from the yellow-plush grandees to the maids in the basement and the attics. Apoplectic might have been the response.

With decimalisation, which we are spelling with an 's' while a 'zed' is demanded for demonetization, purchasing power will slide still further on the road to ruin for pensioners and owners of fixed incomes. The coppers have long been casualties. I am old enough to remember the satisfaction of boyhood's appetite with a farthing as well as a ha'penny bun. The former was not much of a munch, but the latter was quite something. Both had some currants in them and were made with flour which had flavour now completely absent from the products of the technological bakery and its miracle loaf. There was once for children a covetable 'Saturday Penny' in the undemonetized days. A penny!

Denizen

Those vexed persons who discharge their wrath in unsolicited communications to the press take a poor view of the word denizen which originally had a dignified status. It meant a native as opposed to a foreigner. By an Elizabethan statute an alien could be admitted to English citizenship by royal letters patent; he was then said to be denizened. For inhabitants of the sky there was exaltation in the word. Sir Walter Scott called eagles 'winged denizens of the crags'. Loftier still angels were 'the denizens of heaven'. The decline and fall of denizenship may have begun when Southey wrote that 'cholera is denizened among us'.

Now the indignant use the term to signify pestilent infestation. If the complainant hates journalists they are 'the denizens of Fleet Street'. Why not employ the old name of the Fleet Ditch to emphasise the squalor of the poisoned pens? If civil servants are the objects of loathing they are 'the denizens of Whitehall'. When hatred and contempt are being voiced the word horde is usually included. The civil servants descend on us in hordes and hordes have never been angelic. They began as 'plundering nomads', savage and brutish. I live in Hampstead whose householders were once thought of as solid family folk and stuffily conventional fuddy-duddies. But now when I see Hampstead mentioned, especially by Peter Simple in the *Daily Telegraph*, it is taken to be the headquarters of the protest industry with a horde of the tousled, tumultuous 'bed-sitter' denizens whom that impenitent conservative entertainingly derides.

Depolarisation

Polarity is 'the quality of having magnetically or electrically negative and positive ends, magnetic influence, tendency towards a particular direction'. So far, so scientific. But polarisation is now a vogue word for any kind of separation of people and things which could commonly be described as 'poles asunder'. The sociologists, whose contributions to the English language of the lecture-room are more weighty than attractive, have adopted it in both its positive and negative form. Divided we are polarised. United we are depolarised.

A director of 'Community Studies', in an address to the British Association, has been forecasting the future of what is now called unisex. He did not mean that there would no longer be a difference of physical organs; he was not prophesying that our descendants will be hermaphrodites to a man—or half-man. He was only considering the increased resemblance, which he chose to call depolarisation, of men and women. He assumed that those who look alike will act alike. It has been obvious for some time that, if both sexes wear trousers and let their hair flop over their eyes in front, down their necks and round their cheeks, with the frequent facial concealment provided by large and dark spectacles, they will be hard to distinguish. There is similarity of occupation and equal pay for equal work is promised where not already achieved. The wife goes out to work, if her family cares allow, and the husband likes to be something of a cook and shares, though he may not like it, in washing-up. To announce on a professional platform the arrival of the unisex explosion is to obtain publicity in the popular press. All sorts of things explode nowadays.

The speaker did not foresee the disappearance of

normal motherhood as the unisex supplants the bi-sex world. But, with the onward march of genetic chemistry, the test-tube baby may become the usual addition to the population with consequent changes in the way of life. The sociologist on the dais or at the desk is unlikely to talk of altered habits. For him there will be an escalating readjustment of behavioural procedure among the men and women depolarised.

Further comments on the forward march of unisex come from Professor Charles Winick, author of *'The New People: Desexualisation in American Life.'* In an article in *The American Humanist* he maintains that 'as sex becomes increasingly depolarised its ability to excite and incite is likely to decline'.

After this announcement of the obvious he argues that 'the huge circulation of "peep" magazines like *Playboy* and *Confidential* shows that Americans are more interested in looking than doing'. (Cannot these guys combine their exercises?) I then read that 'Of the many pop-sociological descriptions of the period since the end of the last war the most apt is the Age of Voyeurism'. So those concerned about the population explosion need not worry. Peeping Tom, it seems, is not committing the nuisance of paternity. I wonder what those of his girl-friends who are not sexually depolarised think of their status as 'an eyeful' and nothing more. I leave that to the pundits of pop-sociological profundity.

Dickensian

That a man's name should be turned into an adjective of frequent use is usually a compliment to his achievements. I am constantly seeing the word Dickensian. It is usually and reasonably applied to the unpleasant or repulsive things which he so powerfully described.

The London fogs have diminished but, if they return, they are called Dickensian. So too are poverty, slums and squalor. Other novelists of renown have not been thus honoured with an epithet for epitaph. I cannot remember seeing Thackerayan applied to a place or a character or Scottian attached to a Midlothian view or a Border landscape. An English vicarage or country house is not called Trollopian or Austenian. Nor is a Yorkshire blend of fells and factories where the mills run into the moors alluded to as Brontëan or Priestleyan though in all these cases there has been masterly description of the locals in their localities and evocation of the atmosphere. Dickens is always with us and deserves the perpetuity.

That happens especially at Christmas-time. And then the adjective is curiously inept, especially when people talk of 'a regular Dickens Christmas'. There was, of course, a gush of sentiment about the amiable Christmas spirit in the short stories and collected journalism. But Dickens was thinking of a single day when there was heavy feasting followed by home-made fun and games among the families who could afford a big blow-out. Even the poorest did not do badly. Bob Cratchit who kept a family on fifteen shillings a week could buy a goose.

Bob expected to be at work at nine o'clock next morning. That is the important point. If people got 'a Dickens Christmas' now they would have a shock sufficient to cause a General Strike. Our Christmas spreads over most of a week. For Dickens it was a single day. There was no Boxing Day. Bank Holidays were unknown until 1872. For many shopkeepers there was only half a day. On the Christmas morning described in *A Christmas Carol* the food shops were kept busy by last-minute purchasers and the bakers were much engaged in roasting the joints and birds brought along to them.

There were no Christmas cards until 1846. There were no crackers on the dining-table. There were few Christmas presents—except trinkets for children. The unforgettable gathering at Dingley Dell was not a Christmas party but a wedding party which happened at that time. The gifts were for the bride. The Pickwickians did not arrive with an array of presents for the Wardles. Despite the astonishing mixture of accidents on and under the ice and the ample alcoholic consolations they were up and about and soon away next morning on the top of, not inside, a coach despite the freezing weather. So let us drop this nonsense about a Dickensian Christmas. Most people would hate so brief a holiday if they got it. The boss as well as the staff would have to be at the office on Boxing Day, immoderately queasy, no doubt, but moderately and painfully punctual.

Duffery

'To me it is terrible duffery.' So wrote Charles Dickens privately after a visit to the Great Exhibition of 1851. He expressed this disappointment in a letter. As a public statement it would have been poorly received at Buckingham Palace. To the Queen it had been 'the most *beautiful* and *imposing* and touching spectacle ever seen and the triumph of my beloved Albert ... it was his great conception, *his* own and my *own* dear country *showed* she was worthy of it. The triumph is immense!' Duffery indeed!

Dickens, delighting in his amateur acting and a happily applauded professional in his mastery of dramatic readings, was a supreme exhibitionist in

one sense but exhibitions to be visited and scrutin-
ised provided a labour beyond his endurance. Even
the display of sculptured figures of Oliver Twist
and Little Nell did not reconcile him to quite a
short stay in the Crystal Palace in Hyde Park. 'I
have a natural horror of sights', he said. 'The
fusion of so many has not decreased it.' He said
nothing of aural affliction. No doubt he had fled
before an outburst on the great organ, which 'ac-
companied by a fine and powerful wind-instru-
ment called the Sommerophone was a joy to
Victoria'. Information about the sommerophone is
not easily discovered. Whether Dickens had or had
not heard it he would have said that he had. He
admitted lying on such occasions. If somebody
asked him about a remarkable sight he always said
that he had seen it. 'I say, Yes—because if I don't
I know he'll explain it.'

When he called the Prince Consort's master-
piece of organisation a duffery he could have been
accused of disloyalty as well as churlishness. The
earliest meaning of duffing was faking; the duffer
was then a pedlar making bogus claims for the
articles on his tray or in his pack. There was no
duffing of this kind in the marvels to be seen in
the Great Exhibition. Dickens must have been
using some comparatively recent slang. Duff as a
form of dough, yielding Plum Duff, had long been
familiar. In the eighteen-forties the lumpiness was
applied in slang to clumsiness of hand and slow-
ness of mind. The duffer had arrived and with
him the duffery which Dickens considered to be
the result of the Great Exhibition.

Dungeon

When Dr Johnson and Boswell were in the isle of
Mull they were entertained at Moy by the Laird of
Lochbuy whose wife offered them a curious breakfast dish. 'Do you choose any cold sheep's-head?'
she inquired and continued her invitation after
one refusal. The Doctor had been very weary the
night before and had not emerged from his bed
in the temper befitting a courteous guest. Boswell
related that he first declined the cold mutton in a
tone of surprise and anger. Then when the delicacy was again pressed on him, 'he confirmed his
answer in a way not to be misunderstood'. Boswell
was complacently amused since he knew what the
reply would be. The hostess was rebuffed but still
a respectful admirer of her visitor. She called the
Doctor 'a dungeon of wit' which Boswell described
as 'a very common phrase in Scotland to express a
profoundness of intellect'. By common he presumably meant general not vulgar. The local doctor
had just called Johnson 'a hogshead of sense'. The
dungeon seems to provide a better image.

Lady Lochbuy, following the national usage, was
probably thinking of the word dungeon's original
meaning. The French word donjon was a form of
dominion and the building was a lord's turret
before it became a deep, dank cell. A dungeon
could be 'a noble tour' in Chaucer's time. So the
wife of the Laird of Moy was seeing the Doctor
as a massive height of sagacity which indeed he
was. During my Scottish travel I have never heard
any friend or member of a learned company called
a dungeon of wit, which meant a pinnacle of wisdom
in the Hebrides in 1773. But I have met those who
deserved the compliment which now seems as unusual as cold sheep's-head on the breakfast menu.

E

Erogenous

Oxford prefers the form erogenic as an adjective for people and things, garments or the lack of them, which 'excite sexual desire'. The word has recently become fashionable in the vocabulary of fashion. The couturiers have to keep the mode on the move to prevent stagnation in their business. Eros too must be kept in mind. So they ponder over what are called the 'shifting erogenous zones' of the human body.

The geography of physical attraction and permissible exposure has had remarkable shiftings. The Elizabethans and Jacobeans thought that the masculine libido was breast-fed. A lady of quality could reveal much of her bosom but nothing of her legs above the feet. But royalty broke the rule. In the Court Masques the women wore dresses of unusual brevity. Queen Anne, the gay, extravagant and exhibitionist Consort of James I, astonished one of her courtiers. After seeing her appearance as Pallas Athene in Daniel's *Vision of the Twelve Goddesses* he wrote 'now we might see that a woman had both feet and legs which I never knew before'.

The zoning, a word which the town-planners share with haute couture, went up and down. At the Court of Charles II the feminine bosom was much revealed for erogenous reasons and the ankle not at all. The silk stocking had been favoured but not displayed by Queen Elizabeth, who danced under handicap. The Victorians were anti-zone. They carried the 'maxi' dress to the maximum of concealment. But the urge to stimulate was not thereby completely frustrated. There is always curiosity. To hide is to provoke. Now that all zones are on view in public theatres and not only in strip-tease establishments, it may be discovered that nudity is a bore. Whatever may be the next caprice in zoning, Eros will not be out of work.

Exclusivity

I have been privileged with an invitation to become a Charter Member, obviously no common fellow, of Britain's 'most exclusive Key Club'. Its promoters, who stress the noun exclusivity and pay me a great compliment by not 'including me out' of its chartered fraternity, are promising a generous inclusivity in the list of pleasures available. Rich indeed is the vocabulary of hedonism provided in a full flood of admen's English and P.R.P. (public relations prose). Their brochure is broshering *de luxe*.

I am to find, deep 'in the heart of Mayfair', 'an entirely new entertainment concept in the swinging 24-hour cycle of Club life'. There will be 'steerburger snacks', a delicacy new to me, in the Speakeasy. There will be the 'romantic, candle-lit retreat of the Piano Bar to the stroboscopic pitch and excitement of the discothèque with dancing to Soul, Pop, Trad or Jazz'. If I am weary of stroboscopy and the soulful frugging which it stimulates I can 'disappear with my date to the darkest and sexiest cocktail bar in town'. But my date and I will not be altogether lonely. 'Wherever you go and whatever you do there will be an array of beautiful young Pets sensuously attired in velvet and lace' to ensure that my guests and I 'relax in an atmosphere of fun, friendship, and pasha-like comfort'. Such are to be the joys of this inclusive exclusivity.

I should, I suppose, know more about the melodious flow of soul. As a prospective member I must strive to comprehend the proffered bliss of 'stroboscopic pitch'. Research as well as sumptuous expectation is encouraged. So to my dictionary. The Greek 'strobos' meant 'a twisting or whirling round' and its 'scope' is 'a scientific toy which produces the illusion of motion viewed through the openings of a revolving disc'. Once in a lexicon there is always curious company for the word investigated and my further education is advanced by the knowledge that a strobilus is 'a fir cone' or in cryptograms 'an aggregation of sporophylls resembling a fir-cone'. But a strobula has menace. 'It is a segmented tape-worm consisting of a scolex and a chain of proglottides.'

One turns for relief to the consumption of steerburgers, the company of Pets, and the status of a pasha. I think that the experts in public relations prose should have made it bashaw, the eighteenth-century version and a nicely resonant title for the nabobs who had held the gorgeous east in fee.

There is sometimes a little inconsistency in the allurements advertised. In the 'Speakeasy-cum-Rumpus-room' there is 'the boozy hamburger-and-chips setting of America's most chaotic and uninhibited Era'. But elsewhere exclusivity reigns in a 'discriminating hub of London's executive community'. No writer of P.R.P. could vulgarly mention businessmen. Nor could he omit orientation. If the steerburgers and hamburgers are from the west the 'ambiance' is 'British-orientated'.

I would criticise the introduction of such school-girl English as 'fabulous' and 'super-glamorous'.

In the style, however, is the description of this 'pleasure-dome' with its separate rooms described as 'self-contained environmental units'. It was surprising to find so hum-drum a term as 'nightery' introduced. That to me suggests a sleazy joint in Soho, not a palace for pashas in Mayfair. But the joy does not cease with the ending of the night. The premises will be of diurnal use. Could one call it a nighterycum-dairy? There is no mention of a milk-bar, but doubtless the sufferers from gastric ulcers, a malady most incident to executives, can quench their pains and obey the admen's counsel to drink a pintamilka-day. The odd word dairy, incidentally, is derived from the feminine ministrants of the milking-shed. 'Middle-English deierie from Dey, female servant.' If 'a-pinta' be on order it will surely be delivered by a Pet, with proper exclusivity if the consumer be ashamed of so meek a tipple.

F

Fey

In his recently published profile of Robert Louis Stevenson Sir Compton Mackenzie discussed a worry which frequently beset R.L.S. He was frightened of diminishing fertility as a story-teller. Why should he fret? Quality apart, how many invalids who died before they were forty-five have done as much? His desiccation was of the lean body not the lively brain. He knew he would not last. Sir Compton added: 'I think he was fey and let me take this opportunity to protest against the misuse of that word. Fey means 'fated to die' and has nothing to do with fairyland.' This counsel is unlikely to prevail. The menacing fey and the sentimental fairy-fay have become inextricably mixed. Fairy was once a music-hall name for a pretty girl. So it occurred in one remarkably absurd chorus:

> Oh the fairies, oh the fairies,
> Nothing but splendour
> And feminine gender!

The gender has been altered or, in the curiously classical lingo of the 'drag' comedians, transvested. The fairy of slang is now 'a queer'. To muddle him with a death-struck man is odious or (see my first note in this book) abhominable.

Flash and Flash House

This word has had an astonishing number of meanings. It has been both a sudden shaft or blaze of light and a swift movement of water, a spurt, a wave. Surf-riding bathers could once have been called flash folk. Flashes or flashers were for a long time the dandies and fops. Now we speak of Flash Harry for a cheap type of dressy exhibitionist. Why the Harries should have been selected for types of flashiness is no more explicable than the attribution of cleverness to the Dicks.

The ostentatious bucks and beaux were not flattered when the noun was also made a label for thieves, tramps and prostitutes. J. B. Priestley in his history of the Regency period called *The Prince of Pleasure* mentioned the debauched squalor of 'the flash house' as it was then called. In 1817 a Select Committee of the House of Commons investigated the condition of the London police and the criminals with whom they were inadequately coping. In the Regency flash house were boarded and trained for thieving and prostitution large numbers of boys and girls, derelict or unwanted children. The district of St Giles was notorious for these barracks in one of which slept four hundred apprentices to vice. Fagin's den, as Mr Priestley points out, 'was probably a surviving flash house though Dickens could not describe all that went on there'. The boys went the way of Fagin's pupils; the girls were sent on the streets at thirteen or fourteen. The owners of the flash house and exploiters of its inmates could collect a lot of money. The police too, it was made plain in the report, could take their share by accepting bribes for failing to notice such an establishment or threatening its proprietor with prosecution. In this kind of flash we have moved a long way from the sparkling and cleansing sea-waves and river's water foaming over a weir.

Flippant

Cowper called the squirrel flippant. The adjective is now so commonly applied to bantering or facetious chatter that the earlier meaning of flip, to move nimbly, has been forgotten. We should hardly speak now of a ballerina as exquisitely flippant. It is a fair guess that the flibbertigibbet, first meaning a gossiping or flighty woman, began with flipperty as its first half. She flipped her tongue and did not yet qualify as the foul fiend which Shakespeare so named.

Flip has recently been given a 'sexy' relevance. A recent and very successful comedy about amorous pairings was called *The Flip Side*. The characters in the piece had mobile affections. But all, if I remember rightly, was innocent in the end. The flipping was more talkative than sinful. But when we hear in slang of 'a flipping nuisance' the adjective is presumably a polite evasion of a once unpardonable word. I prefer my flippancy to be that of the squirrel of which in the grey species I see plenty in the nearby London gardens.

Flocculent

Flocculence, woolliness, sounds like a serious disease and, as a form of speech, it is an endemic affliction of politics. But on platforms it is more tiresome than lethal. The word has the right smack of contempt in its sound but it is less commonly used than it should be. I would like to hear of some Front Bench dealer in cumbrous double-talk attacked for his insipid and evasive flocculence.

The fleecy stuff makes another regular appearance in 'Letters to the Editor'. I have just read one of these irate communications in which a Minister (or was it the entire Cabinet?) was warned that he or they could no longer pull wool over the eyes of the public. This kind of flocculation seems a curious and complicated performance. Who ever did pull wool over anybody's eyes? When and where did this form of optical traction begin? One thing is certain. Wool-pulling has become a permanent resident in the cliché country.

Waffling is an effective description of the vague official explanation which clears up nothing. It contains the linking of f and l which has long been favoured in the language of contemptuous dismissal and denunciation. The flabby, flaccid, flustered politician, possibly so flummoxed as to be flabbergasted, is floundering in a fix and seeks to escape with a flux of fluffy flatulent flap-doodle. If he maintains a brassy self-confidence he is praised for being unflappable. He may extricate himself by talking flim-flam or flummery. The latter was originally a mixture of oatmeal and wheatmeal which suggests a solid form of breakfast food and a substantial start for the day. But it has been degraded, probably because of its initial letters, to mean empty talk and idle promises. Flummery can be mixed with flattery as well as with face-saving in Parliament. In any case it will be fluent and flocculent, a form of palaver which has been well given the slang name of flannel.

A helpful friend has reminded me that there is a verb floccipend, meaning to dismiss as muddled, woolly and worthless. Sir Walter Scott had a curious fancy for a formidable mass of syllables in the word flocci-pauci-nihili-pilification. Oxford adds to this '*See* Eton Latin Grammar'. My education was not so exalted and I do not possess the book mentioned. The 'pili' part of the monster indicates hairiness and so brings us back to wool, flannel and the rest of the flocculent company. Incidentally, a flocculate person is one who has a conspicuous curl or tussock on his head. G. K. Chesterton dedicating *The Man Who was Thursday* to E. C. Bentley, deplored the decadence of the eighteen-nineties when 'Science announced nonentity and art admired decay'. Contrasted with the darkness was 'the white lock of Whistler that lit our aimless gloom'.

There was a great and gleaming flocculate at large in Chelsea.

Fogey

At my age you wonder what people are calling you. Old fogey, old buffer, old codger, old dotard, old fool? One can in fact be a young buffer since the word only means a silly fellow and such juveniles there are. Buffers, when matured, can be jolly as well as old. But for the fogey no specification of age is needed. He is inescapably senile, 'a man advanced in life with antiquated notions, an old-fashioned fellow'. As a member of this species I accept the definition while maintaining that old notions are not inevitably nonsensical. There are thinkers who advance to the Left with years. When I wrote this Bertrand Russell was ninety-seven.

But I do not like the derivation of my class-name since it comes from the fog which is old rank grass or shaggy moss. Perhaps the first he-ancients to be called fogeys were conspicuously mossy on the scalp, chin and cheeks, but most of the ancients in my acquaintance are free of the fungus which provided the derisive title.

There is no hope for the dotard. That was once the name of a decaying tree which has lost its branches. In his human form the dotard is curtly dismissed in the dictionary. He is 'imbecile', which incidentally meant 'weak of body' before it was applied to feebleness of mind. The dotard is also 'in his second childhood'. To associate dementia with childhood is hard on the boys and girls of today, many of whom are as mentally spry and well-informed as most of their elders. In the family and schools competitive quiz programmes frequently heard and seen on television screens the youngest are impressively precocious and surprisingly omniscient.

A codger is not bound to be a veteran. He began in triplicate as either a codger, a miser or a tramp. He has never been thought of as one who would now be called a nut-case or a nit-wit. With the adjective old prefixed he rose in the world, like the buffer, to be spoken of as jolly. But a fogey is never acceptable in jovial company. He grumbles about the present and is a bore about the past. He repeats himself and vexes the ear with a thrice-told tale. He is an old fool. Much is said about old fools and young fools. Are there never any middle-aged fools meandering on their way to the melancholy condition of a senile clot? I have known some, not yet fogeys, who were fatuous at forty.

Foozle

The word is familiar for a complete mis-hit on the golf course. The frustrated and fuming player will not have his anger appeased by the information that he is talking German in which tongue fuseln means to make a mess of one's work. Whatever its source it speaks aptly for the bungled drive which keeps the ball earth-bound and ending its brief journey in the roughest of 'the rough'. Since 'prone' is now a common adjectival attachment to nouns indicating disaster we may speak of players incurably foozle-prone.

Such an one was that indomitable foozler, Sir John Squire, excellent as journalist, editor and poet (of a school now derided). He had a charming hand in the use of words, an alarming one in the driver's seat of a car and a calamitous one in the manage of a golfer's implements. He was as kindly as incompetent on the tee. Where I used to play he would constantly enter for the monthly medal, foozle his way over the full eighteen holes and then return his card recording a hundred and forty strokes. The winning figure would be about seventy. That was frequently the score made by another high-spirited journalist, Archie Macdonnell, who was a faultless golfer. I asked Squire why he bothered to put in his card. He answered, 'Because it makes things so much nicer for the fellow who would have been bottom.' Could a foozler be more benignant?

I have been reminded by Dame Daphne du

Maurier that in her childhood foozle was a family name for a spot on the face. It was employed by her father, the brilliant Sir Gerald. The Scots for a pimple is a pluke or plook. Here is another picturesque name for the facial blot. It is kinder perhaps to talk of a pimple than of a foozle or a pluke.

Forsythia

When 'Spring blesses us with surprise' we are much beholden to William Forsyth, a Superintendent of Royal Parks, who introduced his 'Chinese deciduous shrub of rambling habits' to shower its golden rain so early and so richly on suburban gardens. Only in Albania has it become a European native. For this impetuous alien, whose flower precedes the leaf, my thanks to Mr Forsyth whom I take to be one of those Scottish gardeners who have been such decorators of the English, and especially the London, scene.

To perpetuate one's name it is best to be horticultural. To import or originate one of 'the darling buds of May', or better still, of March, is to win an enduring place in the flower-books, the dictionaries and the hearts of those who, with the gay products of their green fingers and greenhouses, splash natural colour on the grey surface of the town. Among the 'pacts and sects of great ones that ebb and flow by the moon' the tides of glory wane. A gardener outlives a conquering king. Where now is that lion of the north, Gustavus Adolphus? Herr Dahl, the Swedish creator of the dahlia, is far and wide remembered. Poinsettia we owe to J. R. Poinsett, an American ambassador to Mexico who grafted horticulture on to diplomacy.

After the forsythia, the aubretia, as we wrongly and unfairly call it. I had imagined a cunning

English Mr Aubrey who provided so well for our rock-gardens and borders. I was misled by the common mis-spelling. We have done grave injustice to M. Aubriet, a French artist born in 1743. Henceforward, if I write the word, it shall be correctly as aubrietia.

There are many names thus persisting in a tributary way. Mr Cox whom I have seen located in Bermondsey, is for ever the apple of our palates. Who was Mrs or Miss Perkins, the rose-queen Dorothy? Who the Rev A. Buddle? Unromantically named, he may not have risen to a deanery or a palace, but his soaring buddleia, the 'Orange Ball Tree from Chili and Peru' has given him more lasting fame than comes to many a powerful preacher or theological tycoon. I like to think of him as achieving the archidiaconal rank, the Venerable A. Buddle.

Frump

'They voted me a prig, a frump, and a fogram,' wrote William Godwin, Shelley's father-in-law. Fogram was presumably his form of fogey. It seems a very odd name to apply to one who was an agnostic anarchist; however, he lived to be eighty, which may have caused this contemptuous relegation to fogeydom. Those who called him frumpish were not necessarily thinking of one who looked shabby and dressed in a slatternly way. Now a frump is usually feminine, an 'old bag' in modern slang. But to judge by some of the young University women to be seen demonstrating these days there can be young frumps.

The word started with a very different meaning. It was a flout, a jeer or a sulky disposition. There was a verb, to frump, meaning to mock or insult. Verb or noun, it well describes churlishness in either

71

sex but it is the elder and unkempt woman who has recently been loaded with the name. Is this frump also a harridan? That creature is described as 'a haggard old woman'. She frumps with a sharp tongue. She is also defined as a vixen (possible slander of a good maternal fox?) and that most deject of creatures 'a decayed strumpet'. With that sad and sordid label one sees her in a playbill of the seventeenth century.

G

Glede and Windhover

Christopher Smart's 'Song to David' was an astonishing explosion of exulting enthusiasm in the proper sense of that word—supernatural inspiration or God-given ecstacy. A romantic amid the smooth moods and polished poetical measures of the Age of Reason he was enraptured by the huge and the strange, the bright, the violent and the flashing manifestations of the life force, creative evolution to Bernard Shaw, the works of Jehovah to whom Smart cried hosanna:

> Strong is the horse upon his speed
> Strong in pursuit the rapid glede
> Which makes at once his game.
> Strong the tall ostrich on the ground,
> Strong thro' the turbulent profound
> Shoots Xiphias to his aim.

The glede was a name for the peregrine falcon which swoops on its prey through the air as Xiphias, the sword-fish, darts through the water. Smart was little concerned about their victims, while he was giving thanks for the might and majesty of the animal and avian predators.

Nor was Gerard Manley Hopkins who, no less enthusiastic in his religion, sang the praise of another raptor, the picturesquely and accurately named windhover, more commonly known as the kestrel, a cousin of the glede whom he saluted as 'daylight's dauphin, dapple-dawn-drawn Falcon':

My heart in hiding
Stirred for a bird—the achieve of, the mastery of the thing!
Brute beauty and valour and act, or, air, pride, plume here
Buckle! And the fire that breaks from thee then, a billion
Times told lovelier, more dangerous, O my chevalier!

There is no mention of the field-mouse who was the chevalier's tit-bit.

By a curious coincidence glede also means a warm, glowing coal. Fire flames in the imagery of both men as it did for Blake with his bright-burning tiger. In Smart's zoological panorama:

Strong is the lion—like a coal
His eyeball—like a bastion's mole
His chest against the foes.

To be thus rhapsodical paid no dividends for either man in his time. Smart, although he had at first enjoyed the patronage of a duchess, died at the age of forty-nine in a debtor's prison after being confined as a lunatic.

Hopkins has been thought to suffer from 'acute

73

neurosis'. His confinement was self-chosen, in religious retreats. When he died of typhoid at forty-five in 1889 he had yet to be acclaimed. But when appraisal came it was unstinted in some quarters and recent critics have debated whether he was 'a great lesser poet' or 'a lesser great poet'. Either way, his love for dappled and 'a-dazzle' things, including 'rose-moled stippled trout' and 'fresh, firecoal-chestnut-falls' has not been transient in his readers' affection. The windhover, like Smart's glede, is still on the wing.

Grotesque

'Wordsworth, Tennyson and Browning: or Pure, Ornate and Grotesque Art in English poetry.' Thus Walter Bagehot. The summary judgment would be generally taken as moderately accurate, though Tennyson was not always ornate. One may wonder what Bagehot meant by grotesque. The termination '-esque' implies 'resemblance in style or characteristics', as in arabesque. Therefore it is natural to assume that the cavern or grotto created an adjective for strangeness. But grotesque seems to have begun life as the French crotesque. Later presumably it was associated with the hole in the rocks and its eerie darkness.

The first use of crotesque or grotesque was as a noun describing a form of decorative painting in which animal and foliage forms were curiously interwoven. That was fantastic but not frightening. Then the grotto came into it and the noun was father of an adjective which has come to mean exceptionally strange. Horace Walpole applied it to gargoyles. Later the adjective fathered a verb meaning to exaggerate or caricature. Now the epithet is loosely applied to anything excessive or bizarre.

The cavernous grotto came from an Italian form of the Latin and Greek crypt, a hidden place. In the crypt of St Paul's there is grotesquerie in one of the deposits, the vast sarcophagus of the Duke of Wellington. The grotto vocabulary has included antre from the Latin antrum. Othello's 'travel's history', now doubtless and nastily called his travelogue, included 'antres vast' among the 'rocks and hills whose heads touch heaven'. Shakespeare never mentioned grottoes or grotesques but Milton used the adjective.

The under-world of England's limestone cliffs and hills provides grottoes truly grotesque among which I have wandered in awe at Buxton and in the bowels of the Mendips at Wookey Hole, a superb name for a place of such uncanny quality. In the Pennine fells there is an active and hazardous sport of descending at considerable risk into the narrow tortuous crannies and corridors sometimes flooded after heavy rain. The feckless devotees of these explorations use a language quietly factual and realistic. They are pot-holers not anthrophiles or grottologists.

Golly-Gosh

In a recent television series about a Priory that admirable droll, Derek Nimmo, playing Brother Dominic, a ham-handed novice who touched nothing which he did not knock over, used to exclaim in the presence of the Prior, 'Oh Golly-Gosh!' He was not rebuked for sacrilegious talk by that benign superior to whose patient tolerance Sir Felix Aylmer brought a compelling charm. Yet Golly and Gosh are both escape-words for God and might be regarded as improperly used amid the pieties of this spiritual retreat.

God has been much 'gadded' in the hope to avoid censure for blasphemy from the time of egad and gadzooks to that of golly-gosh and gorblimey. Appeals to Christ have become cripes and crikey and 'Oh Jesus' has been horribly turned to 'Aw Jeeze'. The third member of the Trinity has been less publicly renamed, but I remember from my undergraduate years the jovial son of a parson who had a relish for terms unthinkable in the Rectory. He spoke privately of the Paraclete as the Goggins or the Sacred Spook. If golly and gosh can pass without a rebuke in a priory would 'O Goggins' have been given a black mark if spluttered out by Brother Dominic amid the running taps and broken china of his domestic chores?

H

Hagarene and Other Hags

Amid the racial and seemingly incurable hatreds endemic in Asia Minor it would not gratify an Arab to be told that he had Jewish ancestry and that this came by way of Israel's great patriarch. Meeting and investigating the word hagarene I found that it meant 'a reputed descendant of Hagar, the concubine of Abraham and mother of Ishmael, an Arab, a Saracen'. Tell it not in Gath, mention it not in Cairo, whisper it not on the battle-scarred banks of the Jordan.

Because hagios was the Greek for holy and hag was Old English for a witch, hob-goblin and any ill-favoured or ill-tempered old woman, the confusion of words beginning with hag has been fantastic. 'Her hagship, was a sarcastic way of naming a wrinkled shrew. Yet hagiology is worship of the Saints and a hagioscope is an arch in a chancel wall through which could be seen the elevation of the host. The haggard was an untamed female hawk and then in human form a virago. As an adjective it was used for the lean, hungry and harassed look. The haggis has become a tiresome butt of the anti-Scottish jester but it would surprise him to learn that it was 'a popular English dish before the eighteenth century'.

What is a hagworm? I came across a hill so named while wandering on that lofty, windy and deserted wilderness where Yorkshire, Westmorland and Durham meet beside the foaming waterfall grimly marked on the map as Cauldron Snout. This, I think, must be the loneliest region in our over-crowded England. The place-names of this noble desert between Swaledale, Teesdale and the Vale of Eden with the Cumbrian peaks in view are a symphony of natural desolation and sometimes of man's despair. Here has been the struggle to delve minerals from the rocks and to wrest productive meadows from the sullen moors. Here too is Hagworm Hill.

Was it named after some filthy infester of a sheep's intestines? The hardy Swaledale breed is now the chief source of income for the isolated farmers of this fell country. The more I passed the stones of roofless and deserted homes and looked at my map the closer I came to a history of frustration. The names were a testament of enduring courage in defeat.

They made their own rhyme of ruin. They drove me to a salute and a lamentation in rhyme:

77

Our maps are music and our northern titles,
Like wind among the grass and heather grieve.
Our maps are candid charts of desolation
And wear the Pennine weather on their sleeve.

There's Howl Moor, Wetshaw, Winterings and
    Gutters,
Mirk Fell and Dirty Pool and Hagworm Hill,
Fog Close, Cold Syke, Ravock, and Crooks Altar,
And Loups and Wham and Whaw and Rotten Gill.

Our maps are music and they sing the miners'
Old wrestle with the rocks for yield of lead:
There's Old Gang, Windegg, Eskeleth, and Crackpot,
And Racca Vein, forsaken. They are dead.

Our maps are music and they sing the farmers'
Long battle to wring fodder from the fell:
There's Stony Mea and Nettlepost and Sour Nook,
There's Pasture End and Halfpenny, and Farewell.

Hagworm Hill is in ghoulish company. Crooks
Altar! What a site for the most gruesome of murder
stories!

Happening and Happiness

Hippies have happenings. They are not accidental.
They are contrived stunts or performances, perhaps
gay, perhaps intended to shock. In the language
attached to these antics they can be part of a rave-in
or a freak-out. Not being myself even an occasional,
much less a regular, freaker-out, I gain this information from gossip columns and not by participation
in a crazy happening.

Hippies are droppers-out who would rather see

the world go by than take part in its work. If the organisation of a happening means trouble they have enough energy to manage that. That dropping-out provides happiness is not indicated by the look of those who, weather permitting, sit for hours round the statue of Eros in Piccadilly Circus. A blank look is no evidence of bliss. Anyhow they are not troubled with the labour of washing. That seems to be a rare, unwanted happening.

Happiness is a word which implies an accident. Yet no human state has been so assiduously planned. Pope thought of it as the primary object of man's efforts and ambitions:

> O Happiness! Our being's end and aim,
> Good, pleasure, ease, content!

For it, he added, 'we bear to live and dare to die'.

The hermits, eremites and mystics dropped out of this world to be nearer the next, as Keats understood, when he defined happiness as that

> Which becks
> Our ready mind to fellowship divine,
> A fellowship with essence.

A trance, a vision and a revelation were the happenings in mind. These, imagined by Francis Thompson to be discoverable at Charing Cross, are unlikely to descend on Piccadilly.

Happiness was no accident in the opinion of Robert Louis Stevenson. His puritanical father had for a while regarded him as an atheist without morals or hope of salvation. But he retained some of the inbred ethical austerity and took happiness to be a duty. If not Wordsworth's 'Stern daughter of the voice of God' it was for him the daily obligation of a good fellow. So he wrote:

79

If I have faltered more or less
In the great task of happiness.

We must toil in its pursuit. To the ascetic Bernard
Shaw it was detestable. He spoke for himself through
the mouth of John Tanner in *Man and Superman*.
'A lifetime of happiness! No man on earth could
bear it. It would be hell on earth.'

Whether one shares or spurns the strivings and
raptures of the hedonist the name for his pleasure is
a poor one. Happiness is a sloppy, unsatisfying word.
That may explain the recent vogue for calling it
euphoria. It is not a fashion I follow. If I am to
speak of bliss in classical terms I prefer the Latin
felicity. Says Horatio to the dying Hamlet,

Absent thee from felicity awhile.

Shakespeare's word-sense was infallible.

Honey

Honey was early given the highest honours in both
senses of that adjective. On the lofty summit of
Mount Olympus it was both the food and drink of
the Gods in the Greek fables. It sustained their
bodies and enlivened their spirits. Nectar, 'the sweet
fluid produced by plants and collected by bees' has
survived as a synonym for any delicious drink. It
was the liquor favoured by Zeus and his company
among the crags and the clouds while they feasted
on their ambrosia, whose ingredients are uncertain.
A belief that honey was the root of the matter is indicated by an old English definition of that word as
'bee-bread'.

Ambrosia meant giver of immortality. The pagan
delicacy strangely gave its name to a Christian saint,
an Archbishop of Milan. Boys called Ambrose
should be long-lived. A girl called Ambrosine should

be what is sometimes known as 'a dish'. On nectar and ambrosia the Olympians throve. The myths recording their escapades make it plain that the Gods, and not least Father Zeus himself, were highly sexed and abundantly virile. If the public relations industry had been in action then and promoting a honey market among mortals they had rich material on which to work. Music, as Shakespeare said, may be the food of love. If, in the opinion of the ancients, nectar and bee-bread were so good for the gods, what might not honey do for the amorous types on earth?

The Greeks, having a sweet tooth and being without sugar, used honey to dulcify their dishes and drinks. It sweetened their wine and so may have made it possible to drink more and suffer less on the morning after. That was the Elizabethan belief. Sir Francis Bacon told his readers that 'Wine Sugred inebriateth less than Wine Pure'. Two places on the Mediterranean shores were especially renowned for their honey, Mount Hymettus near Athens and the town of Hybla in Sicily. The English poets were aware of both. From the latter they coined the adjective Hyblaean which appeared in 1614 in the praise of sweet, refreshing things.

Sugar has not been kindly regarded in the language of metaphor and compliment. We do not honour a poet by calling his verse sugary. Nor does that word commend the kind of sentiment so described. But honey has been frequently mentioned in salutes to the finest writing. The contemporary tributes to Shakespeare constantly spoke of his sweetness, not his strength. Francis Meres (1598) loved his 'mellifluous and honey-tongued Muse'. 'Sweet Mr Shakespeare' was the cry of the Cambridge undergraduates in one of their Parnassus plays. 'I'll have his picture in my study,' said one. He was the students' pin-up boy as well as their verbal nectar and bee-bread. So the praise continued. It was honey all the way. The bees were thus honoured with the poet.

That 'lord of language' was constantly mentioning honey and using it in his imagery. The Elizabethans, unlike the ancient Athenians, had sugar at their service, but the poets did not pay it high regard when they used it metaphorically. Sugar stickily adheres to prose. Ophelia, in her glowing praise of Hamlet's qualities said that 'she had sucked the honey of his music vows'. If she had spoken of the sugar of his promises the beauty and the pathos of the line would have completely vanished. 'Death that has sucked the honey of thy breath,' cried Romeo over Juliet, believing her to be dead. It is unthinkable that sugar should take its place in that line. When Shakespeare wrote of 'sugared words' he did so with contempt for flattery and insincerity. When he spoke of 'the sugared game' in *Timon of Athens* (iv. 3) he was describing lust and its legacy of shame and venereal disease. Honey was never thus despised and rejected. For him, with an infallible ear for harmony, honey was the symbol of a gentle and a genuine passion.

The Israelites were extremely honey-conscious. The wild variety made locusts a nourishing diet for John the Baptist. In the Old Testament milk and honey are the tokens of plenty. There is also a striking valuation of honey in the Book of Isaiah. When the prophet was foretelling the coming of a Messiah, he said, 'Butter and honey shall he eat that he may know how to refuse the evil and choose the good.' Was this an ancient warning against the coming of margarine and other substitutes? Plainly Isaiah regarded honey as more than a physical comfort. It was a nourisher of the brain and a stimulant of discretion. That may be nonsense. But if honey is not food for the mind, it has been a great contributor to the harmony of our language.

Hunky-dory

When a gossip-writer reported that Elizabeth Taylor had had what the Scots call a stramash with her equally illustrious husband, Richard Burton, the story was denied. Her agent asserted that there was no serious quarrel and that between them all was hunky-dory. This struck me as odd because the event or non-event took place in Hollywood and not, as one might expect, in Holyrood during the making of a film about Mary Queen of Scots. Hunky-dory is the Scottish vernacular equivalent of O.K., which would have been the more likely usage of this diva's spokesman. I have met the word in Scottish talk and long ago saw in a London theatre a Scottish comedy with that name. I fancy that the title was not helpful. It did not last long. Its author's name was Macdonald Watson, Scottish enough.

In my edition of the *Dictionary of the Scottish Language* edited by John Jamieson, D.D., F.R.S.E., F.S.A., etc., there is no mention of hunky-dory. No doubt it was beneath the notice of that reverend and learned man. He included 'Hunk, a sluttish, indolent woman, a drab' from which sorry class the elegant and industrious Miss Taylor is astronomically miles away. 'To sit on one's hunkers' is explained as 'to sit with the hips hanging downwards,' which suggests excretion. In English a hunks is a surly, crusty and stingy person. In American politics a hunker is or was a stiff and stern conservative. Eric Partridge in the supplement to his *Dictionary of Slang* says that hunky-dory was imported from America about 1938. The statement made by Miss Taylor's agent shows that it is still extant in California, but I think it must have been carried across the Atlantic by the emigrating Scots who found life by no means hunky-dory at home.

I

Interabang

My informative friend, Mr R. D. Franklin, director of the Public Library in Toledo, Ohio, has given me notice of the arrival, which sounds like a detonation, of interabang. This is a proposed addition to the normal series of punctuation terms. Invented by Martin K. Spekter and accepted by the American Type Founders Company, it is a mixture of question-mark and exclamation mark. The excuse for it is the common use of phrases which are both queries and exclamations or mild expletives. 'What the hell,' for example, is cited as deserving an interabang. So, I suppose, is 'What the Devil' and other moans of the frustrated.

The bang comes in from American printers' slang in which it signifies an exclamation point. The suggestion of questionable matter has prompted the editor of the *Harvard University Press Bulletin* to propose that an interabang could suitably appear at the end of many remarks made in pulpits or on political platforms. In this case, when we are told by the highest authorities at the White House or in Downing Street that the affairs of the nation could not be better handled, we may expect some interabanging inserted by cynical sub-editors. That will naturally be followed by protests that journalists are wickedly abusing the freedom of the press by hinting that the preacher, or orator, or public relations spokesman is talking 'flannel'.

Whether Fleet Street will accept this innovation remains to be seen. The device is a mixture of the ordinary question and exclamation marks and not at all conspicuous. The sentence about which the sub-editor feels sceptical will end with a whimper of doubt which is certainly not a big bang. It will need sharp eyesight to notice it. The average reader of reported speeches is usually skimming the text. He is not a specialist in the niceties and subtleties of printing. So if the speaker is interabanged he is unlikely to be given a blow of resounding force. He can take the detonation as no more menacing than the backfire of a motor-car in the street. The children playing with toy guns in the public garden near me are constantly shouting, 'Bang-bang. You're dead.' If the new type-form includes an interabang-bang it is not shooting to kill. It is gently whispering dubiety.

J

Jocund

'Now only literary,' says Oxford. That is true. I do not hear talk of jocundity at a would-be-gay gathering or in the dialogue of a modern play. If it did appear in the latter the critics would scold the dramatist for being literary. That is one of their ad-

jectives of contemptuous dismissal. Should a playwright use any but the drab, overworked vocabulary
of ordinary conversation I see no reason why knowledge and use of literature should be regarded as
vicious. When Christopher Fry was lighting some
verbal fireworks in his unashamedly poetical plays
their radiance delighted me.

Perhaps he deserted the theatre because the
theatre deserted him. Was he not committing this
crime of being literary? T. S. Eliot, the language of
whose poetical plays is scarcely distinguishable from
prose, admitted that his poetry was verbally starved.
It was natural that a piece called *The Cocktail Party*
should not admit adjectives like jocund. A large
Gin-and-it' was not the obvious mixture to be
swigged by his characters and their soul-surgeon pre-
scribing redemption by martyrdom. Nothing jocund
there.

It was surprising to find that epithet applied to
Henry James but there it is in a sonnet of welcome
written to that great novelist by Robert Louis
Stevenson. The 'fair immaculate women' in the
Jamesian society are imagined by R.L.S. walking
'behind their jocund maker'. I find James more
judicious than jocund and would not apply to him
the epithet with which Juliet greeted the new day
poised tip-toe on the misty mountain-tops and which
King Claudius applied to the fierce drinking of the
Danes. For Milton jocundity went with country
dancing on a 'sunshine holyday'.

The presence of the 'y' in holyday saves that description of pastoral jollity from association with the
brochure prose favoured by the merchants of the
packaged tour. The rustic music was that of the
rebeck, a three-stringed fiddle. It was heard among
the Morris capers in 'the chequered shade'. Milton
was not a dedicated sun-worshipper. He did not
sport with Amaryllis in the sun. As a background

setting of happiness he liked 'the fallows grey'. Grey? No artist of the advertising craft, glorifying in prose or paint the allure of the sun-drenched sands by the southern seas, would admit any such sober tint among the blues and golds promised to the packaged family airborne from the towns among the Pennines to a colourful Spanish paradise.

Hilarious is not 'now only literary'. But, however happy the outing, few of the returned travellers from Majorca would tell their friends that their trip had been enriched by constant hilarity. Dr Johnson thought well of that state but warned against seeking it in a bottle. 'Wine gives not light, gay, ideal hilarity, but tumultuous, noisy, clamorous merriment.' The vinous tumult would now be called a rave-in or a wacky ding-dong, words far more suited to liquorish laughter than is the almost prim hilarity. I think of men and women named Hilary as discreet in mirth and not as continual chortlers.

While investigating the vocabulary of fun and frolic I learned something of which I should have been aware in my undergraduate years at Oxford. Why was the name Hilary given to the Lent term of the University and to the Hilary legal sessions? This I had taken without question as I suppose do most people. We owe that description to St Hilary of Poitiers (died A.D. 376) whose Feast Day is on January 13th. Was he hilarious? Was he jocund? Perhaps, but now the date suggests those east-windy weeks and even months to come in which the English climate encourages more comfortable resort to the bottle than supposedly health-giving exercise on misty mountain-tops or fallows grey.

Jug

A nasty little word at first sight but, despite its vernacular connection with clink, nick, stir and the other prison names, it has been attached to beauty in the air and amenity in company. A multitude of young readers have been introduced to poetry with Palgrave's *Golden Treasury*, first published in 1861, and it had been thirty times reprinted by 1903 which is the date of my edition. Having this as their primer the possibily reluctant entrants to Parnassus met on the first page Thomas Nash's Spring Song with its praise of the time when

> Maids dance in a ring
> Cold doth not sting, the pretty birds do sing
> Cuckoo, jug-jug, pu-we, to-witta-woo!

Nash did not name any member of the choir except the cuckoo of whom A. E. Housman unkindly but with some accuracy remarked that it 'shouts at nothing all day long'.

It has strangely been assumed that jug-jug is an echoic reference to the most renowned of avian voices. Oxford is confident about this, 'Jug, to utter a sound like jug, as a nightingale.' In my opinion Philomel does better than that. As a Londoner I have not been able to hear him lately, but when I was some time ago frequently in Surrey I had my casement magically and constantly charmed at night in May and June. Was it only jug-jug, to which 'darkling I listened'? A libel surely that Keats could have resented with no need to censure Nash who was welcoming the season of song with only a single specification. Nightjars are jug-jugglers.

If an Elizabethan girl was named Joan or Joanna she had Jug for a pet name. (Jug of Arc, what a fancy!) Then jug also signified 'a homely woman, maid-servant, sweetheart or mistress'. So almost any woman qualified for the title of little appeal to us. Shakespeare used it only once in this sense. 'Whoop, Jug, I love thee,' cried Lear's Fool when he was audaciously scolding the King for his paternal folly and managing to escape a whipping.

Why jug for gaol? There may, I thought, have been some Latinity here since a captive may be said to be jugate, that is yoked. But the classical explanation is too clever, as Oxford reminds me. Stone-jug was Londoner's slang for Newgate where stone walls did certainly a prison make for the malefactors or unfortunates there bottled up. There, before execution, were jugged among others the throat-slitting criminals who jugulated.

Jug for tuneful nightingales, for winsome Joans, also perhaps for the greasy one who 'keeled the pot' in the exquisite song of the seasons at the end of *Love's Labour's Lost*, jug for the container of refreshing drink to wet the dry jugular section of the drouthy worker, jug as a verb for stewing, especially of hares, jug for the reception of felons. The fools also came into it with one syllable added.

> I'm Billy Muggins
> Commonly known as the Juggins

said the old comic song. If the nightingale may be said to jug-jug he keeps a curiously assorted company.

L

Lackadaisical

Reading of someone who confessed to being lackadaisical and was obviously admitting idleness I was surprised that he chose that curious word. Stupidly I began to think of 'meadows trim with daisies pied' and to wonder why the absence of *bellis perennis* should be connected with the deadly sin of sloth. Basking beside a lawn in summer is the right companion of drowsy dreaming. I should have known that the little flowers which so innocently await the slaughterous approach of the mowing-machine have nothing to do with the sluggard's case.

The lackadaisical person, I discovered, was one who was given to murmuring 'Lackaday' and was therefore, according to Oxford, 'full of vapid feeling or sentimental and affectedly languishing'. I do not remember that Sheridan's Miss Lydia ever used the word which apparently became fashionable with the vapidly emotional in the previous century. Gilbert gave it a still earlier arrival since the date attributed to events in *The Yeoman of the Guard*, or *The Merryman and his Maid*, is 'Sixteenth Century'. Therein Jack Point, the strolling jester, included 'Misery me, lackadaydee' in his ditty of the 'merry-man, moping mum', which was 'Sung to the knell of a churchyard bell'. Was this doleful singer vapid or affected? Rather, I think, he was the usual droll with a heartache, a genuine victim of the cruel command, 'Laugh, clown, laugh.'

Now the lackadaisicals are guiltless of posing. They are just agreeably and impenitently loafing. I can happily be one of their lethargic company, without pretence and with a frank acceptance of the delight of being, at least for a while, comatose.

Literature

'The Grand Cham of Literature.' So Tobias Smollett described Dr Johnson and the title, well applied to the scholarship and the dictatorial manner, became familiar. Now we would think that Smollett had the doctor's writings in mind. But that was not the case. In the eighteenth century literature meant learning and culture in general. This Johnson made plain when he said, 'It is surprising how little literature people have.' He was not referring to a shortage of books. In his dictionary he defined literature as 'learning, skill in letters'.

In his excellent book on *The Rise and Fall of the Man of Letters* John Gross recently alluded to the change from the Georgian scholar to the Victorian bookman writing about books, a type whom one imagines seated at his desk among his packed and massive shelves. He quoted Evelyn Waugh's description of his literary father as 'belonging to a category, like the maiden aunts, that is now almost extinct'. Gross agrees that the term fell into disrepute. There has been a division of the stream of writing. 'Instead of men of letters there are academic experts, mass media, pundits, cultural functionaries.' J. B. Priestley has written novels, plays, essays in great quantity and quality. He has shown the enormous range of his reading and his critical good sense in a large, wide-ranging volume called *Literature and Western*

Man. He is in fact 'a man of letters'. But he is unlikely to be so labelled now and might not care
for it if he was, although Carlyle included that
species in his hero-worship.

There were once the literati, a fine-sounding
name, who resemble Hilaire Belloc's Oxford dons
who

> Sail in amply billowing gown
> Enormous through the Sacred Town,
> Bearing from College to their homes
> Deep cargoes of gigantic tomes.

They were 'compact of port and learning of a sort'.
To me they are literati.

Douglas Young, who combines classical scholarship with a nice mastery of English prose and Scottish poetry, used the term in verses evoked in Edinburgh while he was standing on a wintry day among
the fluted Grecian columns on that city's Calton
Hill. He thought kindly of the 'philhellene' nabobs
and deemed it

> A fine fantasy of the Whig Literati
> To build a modern Athens in our frore islands.

The literati have gone. Their lesser followers were
more amusing than impressive to A. B. Walkley, the
urbane dramatic critic and essayist of *The Times*
in the first quarter of this century, when he used to
write of 'the littery gents'. Walkley, cartooned as
Trotter in Shaw's prologue and epilogue to *Fanny's
First Pay*, is amusingly presented as one of them.

I was reminded of Johnson's definition when I
found it quoted by the well-read but sour, ill-
mannered journalist, Alfred Yule in George Gissing's *New Grub Street*. Yule is a 'littery gent' who
makes a slender living among the famished penmen
in the eighteen-eighties. They grumble, quarrel and
have more malice in their critical tactics than pence

in their pockets. They are not starved of opportunity. The number of magazines which accept literary articles is surprising. If one sinks another bobs up. That does not happen now.

Yule was greedily trying to snaffle his daughter's legacy to start a bookish review with himself as editor, a position of power which he long craved and never reached. The girl had the sense to avert that waste of her small capital. Her father had thought that *Letters* would make a good title. It was a surprising belief that yet another publication of this species and with that name would be supported by a sufficient number of people aspiring to be literate.

Literature, once culture of the mind, has become the written word, usually with an implication of quality. The quantity of 'Eng Lit' amassed has become the embarrassment of overladen librarians and in schools and universities it is the burden of examinees. To it may be attached the mortuary name of a corpus. Below it lies the mass of 'reading matter'. That phrase has an appealing modesty when hundreds of pages of 'interesting reading matter' are being offered. I note that the police are sometimes more polite since, after raiding a smut-shop, they claim to be looking for 'obscene and corrupting literature'. The Johnsonian definition could not be more remote.

Logodaedalism

This is usually taken to mean quibbling because Daedalus was the crafty constructor of the Cretan labyrinth. (Incidental query, why did craft which was a highly respectable name for a profession beget an adjective which usually implies low practice and deceit?) I doubt whether an indignant cry of Logodaedalist was ever heard in Parliament when an embarrassed Minister had given an evasive reply to an awkward question. Perhaps when many Members had some scholarship and classical quotations were familiar at Westminster this taunt may once have reached the Reporters' Gallery.

As an adjective daedal has had a nicer and an ornamental meaning. It was applied to brightly diversified things, especially landscapes. Praising 'The Royal Aspects of the Earth' the Cheshire poet Lord de Tabley wrote aptly of 'the meadow's crest of daedal May'. Consequently the logodaedalist may be one who does not use words to deceive but makes them the material of a rich verbal tapestry. Such an one was the young Max Beerbohm as is explained later under the heading 'Unimpedible'. Dabbing on rare words like paint is not a fashion of authorship or journalism in our time. One sometimes meets it in the public relations prose of the flamboyant advertising man but in that the other kind of daedalist word-juggling is also present. The customer must be caught as well as charmed.

M

Malkin

Australia's Waltzing Matilda was a malkin or the mother of one. Tennyson might have invited a malkin into the garden when and whence the black bat, night, had flown. Malkin is explained as a diminutive form of Matilda and its alternative, Maud. But the malkin's history has been unkind to both these names since it came to mean 'a female spectre or demon', a slut, a lewd woman and a scare-crow. The vision of feminine spite and an equally uncharitable view of the puss turned malkins into cats. If grey, they were called Grimalkin.

For the Elizabethans the 'mini' Matildas and Mauds became menials during their decline to the squalid status of a drab. There is a vivid description in *Coriolanus* (Act II, Scene I) of the crowd awaiting in ecstasy the return of their scarred hero in triumph to the Capitol. He had a reception such as only a pop singer could rely upon today:

> All tongues speak of him, and the bleared sights
> Are spectacled to see him: your prattling nurse
> Into a rapture lets her baby cry
> While she chats him: the kitchen malkin pins
> Her richest lockram 'bout her reechy neck,
> Clamb'ring the walls to eye him ...

A lockram was a rough linen garment. Reechy came from the reek of smoke and so meant dirty. (Shakespeare's Scottish colleague, Laurance Fletcher, whom James I introduced to the Kings' Men, might have called his capital Auld Reechy.) Shakespeare was no equalitarian; he did not see the dignity of labour in the scullery. That was malkin's ground. When he moved on to the brothel scene in *Pericles* the malkin had sunk lower still.

Matilda, though brought to England by the Normans, had an old German and most martial origin. It meant mighty in war. So the kitchen malkin could have been an Amazon violently using the cutlery which she had cleaned, if there were high words and flaring tempers round the sink. Tennyson had not studied the history of Christian names when he wrote of his gentle Maud:

> Her feet have touched the meadows
> And left the daisies pink.

That imprint was not gory, as it might have been in the case of the Germanic Mahtildis, a party perhaps deservedly called a battle-cruiser.

N

Navel

James Bridie, the Scottish dramatist, was less widely known but no less loved as Dr Osborne Mavor. As a medicine man he lectured and wrote delightfully on the human body. In a collected volume of miscellaneous pieces called *Tedious and Brief* (1944) there is preserved an address given to a Glasgow medical Society on the Umbilicus or Navel. 'The word navel,' he said, 'is of absorbing interest. It means the hub of a wheel. Round that umbilicus we rotate. We are both centripetal and centrifugal.'

Umbilicus is a Latin form of the Greek Omphalos which, before the doctors took it over, was a Greek word for the boss of a shield. It was applied to a sacred stone in the temple of Apollo at Delphi which was believed to mark the central part of the Earth. In our own persons its median position has acquired a mystical significance. In the East those seized with a compulsive urge to meditate concentrate upon their physical centre. According to the fancy of Dr

Mavor the navel-gazers murmur as they bow their heads in omphalophilic rapture, 'Om mane padme hum or some such helpful phrase.' For some people there is wisdom in the middle. The belly is as much or even more than the brain. As Gertrude Stein might have put it, 'A boss is a boss is a boss.'

I wonder whether those top-of-the-pop musicians and songsters the Beatles, or one or two of them, when they travelled to India to sit deep in thought at the feet of the wise, dutifully repeated any magic words of the umbilical cult. The product of their contemplation has not, I think, been recorded in a treatise on their pilgrimage. I have long wondered what happens when abstract meditation is practised for many hours on end.

My own occasional efforts in that direction have not been fruitful, perhaps because I neglected my navel. I can think about matters of daily concern, the weather, the work in hand, the Income Tax and the aches and pains inevitable in advancing years. But meditation with no definite subject, 'Thinking High and Thinking Big', defeats me. Coma, which is not unpleasant though not rewarding, is the result. Had I fixed my downcast eyes on my umbilicus in a long and pensive crouch, I do not think that I would have risen a sage. A stiff neck would have been a more likely consequence.

Dr Mavor's omphalic reflections contained much that is both informative and entertaining. They also included some words of comfort for the comatose. 'Man is badly constructed for locomotion. The slowest fish swims faster. He is adapted primarily for rest.' 'He can lie on his back,' the doctor added, 'a posture long sustained by no other uncarapaced animal except in death ... This and much more we can learn from the contemplation of the umbilicus or navel.'

According to Oxford the latter word had a Sanscrit source. But the look of it suggests a link with natal. The boss comes with birth. Whatever its origin it has its place in poetry as a word pleasing to Milton:

> Within the navel of this hideous wood
> A Sorcerer dwells.

Magic and mystery again. Perhaps, if I attempt further meditation in my search for the absolute I should be more centrally concentrated or, in the verbal fashion of today, umbilically orientated.

O

Ouncel

I have been introduced to ouncel by an Irish correspondent. In an obituary appreciation of a vigorous politician, Gerard Sweetman, 'Back-bencher' of the *Irish Times* wrote on January 31st 1970, 'It is one of the conventions at such a tragic time to place on the ouncel the known totality of a man's life so as to come to a judgment as to the man's power and influence on his time and his community, his parliament and his nation.' He later repeats the word ouncel for a weighing-scales in another long sentence. If Back-bencher's prose is to be thus calculated it might be found on the heavy side. Is the totality of a man's life more than the whole of it? But let that pass. I am glad to have met the ouncel, so much more delicate and precise than the ponderous pounder. This scrupulous word appears to be unknown in English dictionaries. Thinking that it may have been taken to America by Irish emigrants I looked for it in the enormous Random House lexicon. It is not there. I have no implement on my desk for weighing letters and small parcels in order to discover what stamps I should attach. If I had I would in future call it my ouncel.

P

Palmiferous

The palm, 'large family of the monocotyledons' i.e. plants with one seed-leaf, has had a curious history. The Romans had made it a guerdon of military prowess. The pious visitants of Jerusalem made it a symbol of a peaceful and successful journey. To bring home a branch was an acknowledged sign of a pilgrimage achieved. Hence the medieval pilgrims were known as holy palmers. My nastily suspicious mind pictures some shabby traders in palm-leaves who did business at the ports with those who had not made the full trip and yet wished to be seen returning palmiferous.

When I won a prize at school, which was not difficult since these Speech Day hand-outs were astonishingly numerous and the competition not at all severe, the book, handsomely bound in leather, carried a Latin inscription. This announced that I was 'bearing the palm' in whatever form or subject I had worked or bluffed my way to the top. It was quite a lucrative field. Books were then cheap. So was leather. The prizes had a stated cash value, sometimes of considerable size. Astonishingly the winners were allowed to choose what they liked from a wide range of authors. Since certain subjects were well endowed by benefactors they were well worth a bit of pot-hunting. Thus I could acquire without much effort the elements of what is called 'a gentleman's library' including more than the conventional classics. H. G. Wells was included. It was a fruitful palm-grove. The victim of this beneficent system was the headmaster who on the inserted label had to fill in by hand the details of every award.

The adjectives palmary and palmiferous are dictionary words. But palm has not always been a complimentary term. The conjurors and the shady gamblers know it. Had I not in my palm-hunting palmed off some shallow stuff on my unexacting pedagogues who were so jaded by the tedium of their task as to welcome a minimum of knowledge displayed by any who knew how to hide their ignorance? To put a few goods quickly in the shop window and conceal what you lack is the secret of the examination business. To win the palm it is necessary to do some palming off.

I wonder whether laurels and bays rank as high as palms in the rewarding routine. They are usually mentioned in a more artistic context. There might have been a Poet Palmate, Palmary or Palmiferous when John Dryden was appointed to be the first official bard and servant of the Crown.

Laurel has been the more popular in the honorific lingo. The eminent must look to their laurels when rivalry is keen or malice active. They are not told to watch their palm. The green bay-tree has been linked with prosperity won by malpractice. The laurels remain unsoiled. Palms, on the other hand, have been avariciously greased, but the dirt was of the hands and not of the monocotyledon. The palm-iferous in my school did not tip the examiners nor did they snatch a previous glance at the questions to be set. That was school-story stuff.

I am reminded that the present and excellent successor to Dryden, Poet Laureate Day Lewis, was after my time a master in the school where I was pursuing the palm. I wish I had had him as my guide on the Parnassus climb. But schools do not always know the talents they employ. He may have been stuck among the maps and formulae of 'Jography and Jometry'. He did well to escape and win the laurel-wreath.

Of previous Laureates Tennyson was the most loyal observer of his official obligations. For royal marriages he duly composed the hymeneal ode. Most familiar is his welcome to Queen Alexandra in 1863 beginning 'Sea-king's daughter from over the sea'. It was followed a year later by 'A Welcome to her Royal Highness, Marie Alexandrovna, Duchess of Edinburgh'. In this there are ten stanzas of five lines in all of which the name Alexandrovna was introduced. It was not an easy undertaking, but the lines came rolling along. They included an optimism which seems excessive. After the wedding would

> Some diviner air
> Breathe through the world and change the hearts of men?

He believed that the hand which carried the royal palm had to beat the drum and Tennyson was an active and accomplished tympanist on state occasions. Would that the human heart was as mutable as he wished.

Palmy days are frequently remembered in the

prose of journalists specialising in sport. The writer may be too young to have seen Jack Hobbs at the wicket or Steve Donoghue in the saddle. But these times are forever a palm-grove to those reporting the best feats of our time. The 'large family of the mono-cotyledons' includes one less agreeable member. Pal-mic means 'of or pertaining to castor-oil'. But here, as with the medieval palmers, we are taken back to the Holy Land. The source of this drastic purge is known as Palma Christi.

Peregrinity

When Dr Johnson was told of a Welsh valley in-habited by Danes who remained distinct and spoke their own language he thought it could not be true. 'These people, sir,' he asserted in his most orotund manner, 'may have somewhat of a peregrinity in their dialect which relation has augmented to a different language.' Boswell challenged him as to the noun employed and got the admission that it had been invented for the occasion. The Doctor added that he had not made more than three or four new words in compiling his dictionary.

Peregrine, meaning a foreigner or traveller, is a formidable Christian name. It may have begun with the pilgrims who visited St Peregrine of Modena, a holy hermit of the eighth century. Naturally it is now often abbreviated to Perry. This diminishes status and authority. The articles in the *Sunday Telegraph* contributed by Mr Peregrine Worsthorne are powerful pieces. Would they seem so important if headed by the curtailed word and denied the full sweep of peregrinity? I fancy not. There is a sound of majesty in the name of the peregrine falcons so called because the hawkers contrived to capture them during migration. English insularity gave a contemptuous ring to the adjective peregrinate. Shakespeare used it so in *Love's Labour's Lost*. The pedantic schoolmaster Holofernes dismissed Don Armado 'the fantastical Spaniard' as too 'picked, too spruce, too affected, too odd and, as it were, too peregrinate'.

Ploy

I like the word ploy for an occupation or a pastime. The *Oxford English Dictionary* defines it as 'Scottish and northern', but it does not appear in Jamieson's *Scottish Dictionary*. Origin obscure, says Oxford, but it plainly looks like a shortening of employment. If a hobby or game is the principal idea in mind it could be a corruption of play.

In an admirable survey of Stephen Potter's life and work as scholar and entertainer Bernard Levin said that Oxford's definition was faulty. I think that it was Potter who gave ploy a new meaning which the *Penguin English Dictionary* accepted, that it is 'a tactical manoeuvre in a game'. Potter, in his notable Guide to '*Gamesmanship, or How to Win Without Actually Cheating*' made ploy a form of cunning. But there was nothing deceptive about a ploy when I first knew it. Words are my pastime-ploy and I have never thought of my wordsmanship, whatever its errors, as a form of low cunning.

Privy

A correspondent writing to me about an autumn walk in a remote part of Dorset, told me of the splendour of the hedges, with 'the bright bryony, spindle berry, hawthorn and the wild black privet so much more distinguished than the cultivated privet hedge'. He added, 'Privet, I see, gets its name from being used in enclosing "privy" gardens.' It was a serviceable shrub when 'extra-mural' sanitation was common, and there were earth-closets among 'the fairies at the bottom of my garden'. In mid-Victorian times there were plenty in the middle of London, even in the Oxford Street area, with no vegetation to conceal them or sweeten the air.

Does anyone talk of a privy in these genteel days of 'the toilet', a name now encouraged among schoolchildren? As an adjective privy has the loftiest associations and precedes Councillors to Her Majesty, a historic Seal and the Royal Purse. I have wondered what was the Victorian slang for this resort of those politely described as 'obeying nature's call'. To say nothing of such needs was part of the silence, not only about sexual practice, imposed upon the novelists. I cannot discover that any of Trollope's characters was ever 'taken short' nor can I see his Duke of Omnium asking hurriedly to be excused from a discussion on his darling topic, decimal coinage, now imposed a century later. But one can think of him as constipated. Of the Barchester folk, only the wretchedly poor 'perpetual curate' of Hogstock in his miserable home can be imagined with a privet-hidden resort. Dickens was no less reticent about washing as well as evacuation. What sort of bathroom had Mr Dombey who might have called his loo his privy?

Prolix and Prolific

Prolix is not an adjective in common use now. We think of a loquacious talker as a gas-bag and of the too verbose or too prolific writer as long-winded. Prolix is a classical dismissal. 'Conscious dullness,' said Dr Johnson, 'has little right to be prolix.' This came oddly from him who for once appeared platitudinous instead of trenchant. The word is linked in origin with liquor and liquidity, suggesting a running tap which needs to be turned off. I trust that in a lifetime of 'scribble, scribble, scribble' I have rarely been prolix. Certainly I did not begin so. When I read a freshman's essay to the Master of my College at Oxford, the courteous but apt comment was, 'Your style, Mr Brown, is a trifle jejune.' The first meaning of that adjective is starved, fasting, hungry and thin. Meagre I may have been, prolix I was not.

A long training in and practice of journalism has certainly discouraged prolixity. A newspaper demands immediacy; if the reader is bored by the first paragraph he readily turns to another report or article. The middle section of my scribbling years came when brevity was rigidly enforced by severe rationing of newsprint. The scarcity is almost incredible now when one sees and possibly shrinks from the massive quantity of the 'quality' Sunday papers, with their various supplements. While I was editing the *Observer* from 1942 to 1948 we had to condense all the wartime news and some views, including criticism of the arts, plus the advertisements into eight pages one week and six the next. Every word had to be watched. Editor and subeditor were tailors and cutters.

Without mercy we trimmed, imposing jejunity on the prolix. Naturally the eminent contributors with big names were effronted. But I am sure they were more readable when reduced in length. Those subject to the scissors and the razor did not like it. But their debarbellated prose was, I am sure, made more readable by the treatment.

The prolific writer need not be prolix. Those whose crime stories appear in a steady flood are not as a rule long-winded. They have an immense capacity for spinning plots but they are not word-spinners. Agatha Christie and Simenon do not go drooling on. To be prolific is to be fertile in ideas and their output. The adjective has no connection with prolixity. It is linked with the fertility of the proletariat which was originally 'the lowest class of the people of ancient Rome who were regarded as contributing nothing to the State but their off-spring'. The prolific writer, spawning books, may add greatly to his income, but is unlikely to do so if he is prolix and provides more wrapping than content.

But my own tap is running on. Let a timely recourse to the jejune turn it off.

Pseudism

Osbert Lancaster in *From Pillar to Post—the Pocket-Lamp of Architecture*, as entertaining in illustration as in text, includes Pseudish among his list of housing-fashions. He described it as 'Pont Street Dutch with a few Stockholm trimmings and a more daring use of colour'. Tiles of a vehement shade of green provide the roof for the whitewashed walls with their artily leaded windows. The vogue for this was upper-class, he decides, and nineteen-twentyish in the date of its popularity. The principal sites were the sea-coast, 'the more exclusive by-passes' and expensive suburbs. (How aloof can a by-pass become?) This kind of architectural assortment did at least give a splash of colour to its various locations, which Tudor-pseudish did not.

Pseudish adds to our vocabulary of shams in an easily understood way. Its companion words are mysterious. Bogus, origin obscure, is said to have come from America. Phoney is also American. It became popular in Britain about thirty years ago when the quiet start to the six years of desperate conflict was called 'the phoney war'. The word may have been an importation of an export. It has been suggested that fawney, an old English slang word for faked jewellery, was taken across the Atlantic by crooks and there got a new look as phoney. Snide had a similar history. It began with the counterfeit jewellers and came to mean tricky in general.

Pseudish might be limited to the arts. There is nothing criminal in its architectural manifestations. We need a franker term for the gab of a televised politician. Phoney or snide for him.

R

Ransack

While I was reluctantly engaged on some tidying up of old papers it occurred to me that the ransack operation, so tedious and interminable, was bringing a strange word into my mind. Why ransack? It came from Old Norse in which tongue it meant seeking for things wanted, and its arrival came nearly five hundred years ago. The Norsemen did some pillaging in the countries which they visited but the old ransackers were not sacking in that sense. They were more tidy than terrible.

We have since had fossicking for these investigations of desks and cupboards. That was originally a gold-miners' term for digging into crevices in search of fragments of treasure. When I fossick I may turn up an old letter of special interest or one which carries a valued signature, but the bundles thus fossicked are mainly a dusty nuisance. The great houses once had their muniment rooms for storage of documents. A muniment was a fortification before it became a title-deed or a collection of family papers. Now most people live in much smaller premises which makes ransacking and removal a frequent necessity. Our muniment rooms are attics which one dreads to investigate because so much old stuff has been stowed away there. In the attic there is not only lumber but a word which has come down in esteem while going up to the top of the house. It should be Athenian and architectural, a lofty 'entablature' in the main façade of a building in the classical style. But now as 'a top storey under the beams of the roof' it is often a pestilent convenience, crammed with the fossickable litter which should have been ransacked years ago.

S

Sir

As a respectful form of address to elder men Sir lingers on. I have even known it as a polite alternative to he. 'Will Sir be coming too?' The person so described by a young friend was myself, who am neither baronet nor knight. A friend of mine told me not long ago that he had ordered his children to call him Sir. I never found out the extent of their compliance but I doubt whether it was frequent. To stress 'the generation gap' in this way is unlikely to be popular.

Sir, applied to commoners, has completely contradictory implications. It can be courteously deferential. It can, according to the dictionary, be 'used with scornful, contemptuous, indignant, or defiant force'. I remember a nice example of the latter which I overheard when I was watching a game of Rugby football. Out of a steaming welter of sixteen players closely and fiercely engaged in what is called a loose scrummage, ruck or maul came a roar of '— you, Sir.'

The Shakespearian Sir was often derisive. One thinks of Sir Pandarus and of Gratiano's pompous wise-acre:

> As who should say, I am Sir Oracle
> And when I ope my lips, let no dog bark.

The incessant Sirring practised by Dr Johnson included respect but was often offensive. 'Sir, I have found you an argument, but I am not obliged to find you an understanding.' Johnson's Sir was a useful trick of his intellectual truculence. He knew that to start a sentence in this way was to begin, as a golfer would say, 'one up'. There may have been times, unreported by Boswell, when a victim could take it no longer and reacted with the explosive Sir of my infuriated footballer.

Slieveen

The far too early death of John Moore was a great loss to English writing especially about the Cotswold countryside of his boyhood and of his enduring affection. In gratitude for his book *These English*

Words a Canadian, Mr Ames, sent to his widow a list of what he called 'Newfie' words current in the 'speak' of Newfoundland. She kindly sent them on to me as one who had welcomed John's collection and enjoyment of dialect.

This fascinating glossary revealed the richly assorted vocabulary of a maritime people whose immigrants had brought with them elements of Scandinavian, French, English, Scottish and especially Irish origin. I hear echoes of the old Abbey Theatre plays in such a word Slieveen, meaning deceitful, an apt description of Synge's immortal *Playboy of the Western World* who in 'Newfie' talk would also be a jackeen. The list includes shooneen for a cowardly fellow. Those critics who nowadays are rather lofty in their attitude to Synge may be said in the 'Newfie' lingo to glauvaun which means 'to complain about trifles'. The Playboy was not only a slieveen; he was a gamogue, a trickster.

He was also, while his reputation as an audacious parricide lasted, plaumashed (flattered) by the colleens but the origin of that word was not explained by our informant. The keeper of the shebeen in the play may have been a gadogue, a fat easygoing person, and a gumbeen who in Newfoundland is a chewer of tobacco. He was no gombeen, a money-lending shop-keeper who liked to keep his customers in debt and so in his power.

The Synge country contained those who in Newfoundland are gammel bostoons, stupid old clots. Is bostoon a slur on the home of learning in whose academic life Dickens discovered 'enthoosymoosy' as a quality of transcendental philosophers? It seems unlikely that the contemptuous users of the word bostoon should be thinking of New England's lofty brows. They have another name for a low-browed person, oonshick. The origin of that is obscure but unlikely to be Irish. If you are puzzled by that you are sharoused. The old English of the first settlers survives in the words for the firewood which they urgently needed. Shakespearian vocabulary lingers on in faddle (Hamlet's fardel) for a bundle and in bavin for brushwood which King Henry IV applied to the wits of the rash jesters 'soon kindled and soon burned'.

Sequacious

I was pleased to be reminded of this word by finding it in a novel of the eighteen-nineties, George Gissing's *Born in Exile*. In it a central figure is Godwin Peak, an odiously priggish and snobbish student at a provincial university college. He comes from a shop-keeping or shop-serving family and is bitterly ashamed of it. In describing with distaste his elder female relatives he describes them as sequacious. The dictionary definition is 'ductile, pliable, and slavish' in following a lead. It is an adjective with a sneer in the sound of it, but rarely used now. A party Whip in the House of Commons might demand more ductility and sequacity from the members whom he chivvies, but he probably has never heard of the latter word.

The derivatives of the Latin sequor (I follow) have had a curious history. The adjective executive was once applied to a man who did what he was told, putting orders into practice. And so he still is if he is executing a will. Now executive is a noun for one who is 'a big noise'. On the 'admin' side of a large business he has become the one who gives orders and considers himself to be very important.

Executive has gone up and obsequious has gone down. It meant properly dutiful before it was degraded to mean cringing. King Claudius, while complaining that Hamlet was persevering too much in 'obstinate condolement' acknowledged 'his filial obligation for some time' to display 'obsequious sorrow'. For no obvious reason obsequies became limited to funeral rites and observances. At one time a coronation could have had its joyous and appropriate displays of obsequious loyalty.

Consequential provides another example of the mutable sequences. It can still signify a natural and appropriate result as in the 'consequential damages' awarded to a successful litigant whose counsel has proved his case for compensation. But the word is frequently applied to a self-important person who, having a position in life, behaves in a way that will make the world aware of it. The copy-writers of advertisements use both executive and consequential as epithets implying dignity or grandeur. A suite of rooms, a desk or a chair is called executive and thus is expected to confer prestige. I have seen a suit of clothes described as consequential. Gentlemen so thought of would never be ductile, pliable or sequacious.

Shooter

I have been given the professional wrestler's way of life and the lingo thereof by a relative who offered a lift in his car to a young man launched on a career of this seemingly traumatic kind. For those who know their way about the arena there may be more gab than strangle. 'Never mix it with a shooter' is one of the professional rules. This means 'Don't wrestle with amateurs because they really hurt each other'. My friend's informant was technically 'a villain'. That is 'a baddy whom the crowd loves to hate'. His opponent is known as 'Blue Eyes'. The villainous one makes 'Blue Eyes' die. 'Dying' is looking as though you were writhing in agony though

112

not in fact hurt at all. The routine makes the man who is down recover from his mimic agony and throw the villain out of the ring. That manoeuvre is so neatly contrived that he lands on the lap of his dolly who is duly waiting to receive him.

My friend was given some instruction. 'In theory,' he wrote, 'I now know how to jump on a supine person's stomach without hurting him, but I have not tried it yet.' The money-earning wrestlers can obviously give a good lesson in histrionic expertise to children playing 'Let's pretend'. If they have a Trade Union it might be a section of Actors' Equity. In other sports there are frequent accusations of 'shamateurism', but when the amateur or 'shooter' gets to grips there is nothing bogus about his contribution to the spectacle. Prudently avoiding such intruders the 'pro' knows how to play the game and 'die', quietly, without distress, and with the final comfort of what cricketers would call 'a dolly catch'.

Sunscapology

This from the brosher (brochure) English of a travel agent inviting me to 'get away from the rat-race'. (I am heartily sick of this rat-race cliché. Who organises rat-races and where could I see one if I wanted to? The idea that everyone who goes to work to earn a living is a pestilent rodent is foolish and offensive.)

Sunscape is a good enough word if the 'ology' appendix is removed. I cannot remember moonscape being applied to the filming and television of the achievements of the astronauts, but it accurately describes the dreary, dusty wilderness which they explored. Seascapes and cloudscapes I have met and intervening sunscapes would brighten the latter.

Should they be skips instead of 'scapes'? Milton wrote in 'L'Allegro':

Streit mine eye hath caught new pleasures
Whilst the Lantskip round it measures,
Russet Lawns, and Fallows Gray,
Where the nibling flocks do stray,
Mountains on whose barren brest
The labouring clouds do often rest:
Meadows trim with Daisies pide,
Shallow Brooks, and Rivers wide.

He did not mention a cloudskip, but had he chosen
to do so he would have probably preferred the English version of the Dutch suffix which prevailed
in his time. In 1656 one who seems to have dis-
approved of Oliver Cromwell called him 'that Land-
skip of iniquity, that Sink of sin, and that Com-
pendium of baseness'.

Rose Macaulay, a devoted Miltonian, liked to
maintain the old form. Landskips for her and I
suppose Sunskips too. In her last years she went on
a cruise to Trebizond. One of her companions told
me that she was extremely nimble, whatever the in-
tensity of the solar rays. The idea of a sun-skipping
tourist, though based on a pun, has its attraction,
but the 'brosher' artists, in their praise of sun-
drenched beaches, usually populate them in their
pictures with nudists blissfully dormant and im-
mobile. Lounging, not leaping, is featured in the
appeal to sunscapologists.

Susurration

Looking eastward to Snowdon rising in a pearly sky
and savouring 'the thymy, turfy, salty air' Sir John
Betjeman in a poem called 'A Bay in Anglesey' recorded the mingling of the aural with the visual
pleasure. In the last line he wrote of the 'sweet
susurration of incoming sea'. He might have used

simpler words like whisper and murmur. He is not a struggling poet who would prefer the longer to the shorter simply for scansion's sake. He must have felt that the gentle plash of the rising tide was indeed susurrant, and that the noun was the right one.

All three words can be classed as echoic. The learned may choose a longer label and call them products of onomatopoesis. Echoic suffices for me since it accurately describes the similarity of the verbal sound to the thing in mind or on view. The echoic has often been linked with alliteration. The susurration in this case has two neighbouring s's. Tide, not sea, could have been the final word, but it was rejected.

The most familiar example of the blending occurs in Tennyson's interminably quoted, because so easily remembered,

> The moan of doves in immemorial elms
> And mumming of innumerable bees.

To get this pattern of b's, l's, m's and r's the honey-tongued Laureate was not being precise in his dendrology, 'the part of botany which treats with trees'. Longevity is not characteristic of the elm which is unlikely to outlive many memories. It decays more rapidly than most and is easily sent crashing by a gale-force wind. Elms by the roadside can be a menace to passing drivers. If Tennyson had put accuracy before melody he would have housed his plaintive doves and set his bee-loud glade among immemorial oaks. But the music of his lines would have suffered. The poet of today has no use for such obvious contrivances and cosseting of the ear. I am sufficiently conservative and senile—fuddy-duddy you may call me—to enjoy them without shame, if employed with discretion and without excess.

Murmur and whisper are both attuned to their

purpose. Music and meaning are in unison. They come to mind when I hear the Hebridean lilt of the Eriskay love-song with its lapping of waves on the island shore, a sweetly sad and gentle susurration. Murmurs in poetry speak of dalliance on drowsy afternoons in high summer among Wordsworth's 'soft eye-music of slow-waving boughs'.

Yet the word has often been used to indicate menace. When the people are murmuring and whispering their rulers may be in danger. Conspiracy has naturally a muted voice. I can never forget that heart-rending line of John Webster's in *The Duchess of Malfi*. When the doomed woman is beset by her plotting and murderous kinsmen she knows what is coming. She craves to be 'out of their whispering'.

The Whispering Gallery was 'a gallery or dome of circular or elliptical form' so designed that listeners in the know and rightly placed could pick up the smallest sound. The lobby of the House of Commons was not constructed for that purpose but it is the home of far-reaching whispers, of ears eager to hear and of pens quick to report. Who's in, who's out? There may be an exclusive story in the air for the adroit journalist. Like the tragic Duchess a Minister with a career at stake would gladly be whisper-free. Susurration is a word so rarely used that it has not gathered any political associations. Westminster is murmurous. It is not susurrant.

Squiddle

The first Lady Granville, the witty and charming wife of Britain's ambassador in several capitals during the first half of the nineteenth century, was a frequent writer of vividly amusing letters. This I learned from the excellent life of Her Excellency written by Mrs Prudence Hannay. When Harriet Granville was presented to the King and Queen of the Netherlands, she described her introduction by 'a little *grande-chambellan* and four *dames* d'honneur' followed by five minutes of 'small Royal talk' with their Majesties. Then, she wrote, 'I back out with a train five yards long, squiddle a little with my *grand-maître* and that is all that belongs to my duties *vis-à-vis* the Court.'

What was this ceremonial squiddling? I can find no explanation. It does not sound attractive. The 'sq' words are usually somewhat unpleasant. It suggests fidgeting, but the Ambassadress was not squiddling alone. It was an activity shared with her lordly escort. Did she exchange compliments or even flirt? If the latter, the account of her career and the liveliness of her pen suggests that this daughter of the glamorous Georgina, Fifth Duchess of Devonshire, could squiddle very prettily. I would welcome information.

Syndrome

'What the hell's a syndrome?' The voice came from one reading his newspaper in a bad light. Syndrome has become a favourite with politicians, economists and the journalists who have to report or discuss their troubles and schemes. The word has been taken from the medicine men who thus nominate 'a concurrence of several symptoms in a disease'. I had first heard of it when I asked the cause of a friend's death. On being told that he had suffered from a syndrome and inquiring what that meant, I was given the sad and simple answer, 'Everything went wrong at once.'

The syndrome about which we read in the more academic sections of the press is a collection of circumstances and conditions which is not necessarily disastrous but usually signifies a general mess, as it does in clinical diagnoses. It is found in the company of other vogue words and phrases such as 'the economic spectrum'. Another of its neighbours may be, 'In the context of the international monetary complex'. A group of buildings, possibly syndromised by a Planning Authority, is an architectural complex in which there is 'integration of functional structures relevant to this day and age'. The exact meaning of syndrome is a running together. A gallop is not the usual pace of the planners, but when government departments seize private property the pace may be rapid. Should one baffled by syndrome also ask, 'What the hell is integration?' The answer may simply be 'grab'.

T

Telegraphese

In 1878, when *Who is He Popenjoy?* was published, Trollope in that book (Chapter 20) paid to his old employer, the Post Office, a remarkable compliment:

the pith and strength of laconic diction has now been taught to us by the self-sacrificing patriotism of the Post Office. We have all felt the vigour of telegrammatic expression, and, even when we

118

do not trust the wire, we employ the force of wiry language. 'Wilt thou be mine?—M.N.' is now the ordinary form of an offer of marriage by post; and the answer seldom goes beyond 'Ever thine— P.Q.'

Trollope also observed that 'fifteen or twenty years ago when telegraph wires were still young and messages were confined to diplomatic secrets, horse-racing and the rise and fall of stocks, lovers used to indulge in rapturous expressions which would run over pages'. His belief that the wires had, even then, made the amorous and ample epistle an antique is questionable. He was surely anticipating the decline and fall of the love-letter. Certainly the fashionable dramatists for some years to come did not agree. The 'scène à faire' of a strong society drama continued to include and to exploit the substantial packet of compromising correspondence which had to be somehow saved from its discovery by a jealous husband or exploitation by a blackmailer on the pounce. The contents of the bundle were frequently spoken of as 'the fatal missives'. For a lover to commit himself on paper at length was still the practice when Oscar Wilde was composing his dramas of the titled folk whose intrigues had to be concealed and whose scandals averted.

The lingo of telegraphese was a useful check on verbosity. A friend of mine, always a financially embarrassed husband, wired to his wife, 'Have borrowed five hundred pounds. We are solvent.' He was not wasting his words or his pence while revealing that his sense of economic balance was curiously sanguine. The Edwardian Poet Laureate was not being long-winded when he wrote 'On the Illness of the Prince of Wales, afterwards Edward VII':

Across the wire the electric message came,
He is not better. He is much the same.

The *Oxford Dictionary of Quotations* denies the certain attribution of this couplet to Alfred Austin and refers to a statement on the matter made by Sir J. Lewis May in the *Dublin Review*, July 1937. Since few people can have the specified issue of that publication at their side (and certainly I have not), it is difficult to decide on the authenticity of Austin's succinct contribution to English poetry. But surely the lines can be found in print in the collected works of that royally honoured bard.

However that may be they could have been claimed by Trollope as evidence of the pith, if not the strength, of the 'laconic diction' taught by the Post Office and its new facilities. The affectionate and sometimes fatal missive was further discontinued by the use of the telephone. I remember a popular song in which the singer lamented this kind of absentee's message:

> With your lips pressed to the telephone
> When they might be pressed to mine.

Yet I suspect that even now there are some love-letters, even 'king-sized' as they say of cigarettes, committed to the post-box.

Tribology

The monstrous ologies continue to add to their number, exploding like the population. Sociology, which had not been heard of as a degree subject in my academic years is prolific in this kind. So inevitably is technology, so classical as well as cumbrous is its language. The once monosyllabic man in the moon has become the talking point of the experts in selenology.

Now comes tribology. The Ministry of Technology, we are told 'has a highly successful Committee' studying and recommending tribological progress. That working party might be expected by untechnological simpletons like myself to be housed by the Foreign Office and engaged in pacifying the new African republics. Not so. It is dealing with mechanical tribulations in the workshop.

In adopting tribology the Ministry was not word-making in a wanton way. It had consulted the lexicographers of the Oxford University Press who accepted the new term. They could hardly refuse, since their dictionary had for some time contained 'tribometer', 'an instrument for estimating sliding friction', based on the Greek words for rubbing and measuring. Those applying 'sliding friction' to our stiff limbs, once known as masseurs and masseuses, now prefer to be called physiotherapists. If they want more syllables to their name, as most skilled persons do, they can be styled practitioners of tribological manipulation.

We are assured that tribology is a good investment for the nation since British industry is said to have been losing more than five hundred million pounds a year through its ignorance of what disasters may happen when sliding surfaces are moving across one another. This kind of trouble can occur, it seems, even in the best of well-regulated larders. Did your refrigerator fail you? Did the solids begin to squirt? There was 'a fault in the region of the compressor'. Tribology to the rescue! The science spreads. There are Tribology Centres in two of the new universities which are expected to pay their way by consultation fees, good news when the tax-payer has to find new millions by the hundred every year for education.

So upward and onward goes the new ology which has a National Centre at the Reactor Engineering Laboratory in the United Kingdom Atomic Engineering Authority. 'There's the rub,' was an old exclamation of the bothered and bewildered, of whom Hamlet was one. It is now the diagnosis of the helpful tribologist who is doing much more than preventing the domestic 'fridge' from being accident-prone as he hunts down superfluous friction wherever things are grinding to a halt.

Truffle

This coveted member of the *tuberaceae* puzzles the seekers of verbal origins. The name comes from France, but why did it sprout there? It makes a satisfying sound, suggesting good eating without the gourmet's fussiness. I thought of this while reading Mr Wyndham Lewis's note in his anthology already mentioned. He had included among the selected contributors to *The Stuffed Owl* the medically and biologically minded Erasmus Darwin (1731–1802) who mingled with his scientific research some poetry in the style and metre of his century.

One of his themes was the capacity of certain plants and creatures to achieve monosexual fertility. This cannot be called parthenogenesis since it is often the male parent who manages to avoid the raptures and the pains of sexual ardour. Beginning with the truffle Erasmus listed some of the self-perpetuating species:

So the lone Truffle, lodged beneath the earth,
Shoots from paternal roots the tuberous birth.
No stamen-males ascend, and breathe above,
No seed-born offspring lives by female love ...
So the male Polypus parental swims,
And branching infants bristle all his limbs.
So the lone Taenia, as he grows, prolongs
His flatten'd form with young adherent throngs;
Unknown to sex the pregnant Oyster swells,
And coral-insects build their radiate shells.

Those in no need of assistance in the maintenance of the breed are a curious company, including the innocence of 'the succulent bivalve', as the old-time journalist used to call the Whitstable or Colchester native, and the formidable octopus of many and bristling limbs. The 'lone taenia' is the solitary, unpartnered but not easily evacuated tape-worm.

As far back as 1930 Mr Wyndham Lewis made this comment:

> It might be justly added that in this age of universal exploitation in print of erotic situations Darwin's tribute to the chastity of the truffle strikes a welcome note.

In the publication and dispersal of erotica the march of progress has become a gallop. What would he say now?

U

Unimpedible

Max Beerbohm, defending and saluting Henry Arthur Jones after a production of *Mrs Dane's Defence* in 1900, chose for the caption of his article 'This Unimpedible Mr Jones'. The adjective has not been noticed, or if noticed, not accepted by the arbiters of the dictionary 'passes'. Yet, if unimpedible does not merit an 'A Level', it surely is good enough for an 'O'. Its meaning is plain. Its sound properly suggests the steady tramp of feet that would not be tired and, in this case, of a hand that would not flag or falter at the desk.

Max was attacking the dramatic arbiters for their continual belittling of H.A.J. while he was 'dwarfing before the public those rivals whom the critics delight to honour'. Pinero was their triumphant man of parts, Jones their plodding manikin. The successor to the likewise unimpedible Bernard Shaw at the *Saturday Review* praised Jones not only for keeping up with himself but also for obstinately keeping on. Hostile notices were no impediment to him. I wonder how the coiner or borrower of this adjective pronounced it. Was there a long 'e' in the third syllable? When I met it, somewhat surprisingly, in print, I first thought of it as rhyming with incredible. But unimpeedible puts the desired stress on the playwright's refusal to be put down. Persistence may sound dull but Tennyson found splendour in its stubbornness. To his comprehensive exultation of 'glory of orator, glory of song' he added 'the glory going on—and still to be'. In the *Idylls of the King* he himself did some going on. With Arthur as his theme he could be unimpedible.

The choice of Max to follow him as theatre critic for the *Saturday Review* was made by Shaw himself. The editor, Frank Harris, was on his way out despite a brilliant choice of staff and the gaining of a new renown for his weekly. He had gone to the South of France when G.B.S. became seriously ill in the spring of 1898. With nobody in supreme authority the musical critic, Runciman, was deputising for the absentee Harris. The most brilliant of the team chose the man to follow him, greeting him as 'the spritely, the incomparable Max'. The adjectives were as just as the action was generous since Max was no Shavian at the time and neatly punctured (he was not one to hammer or bludgeon) the author of *Plays Unpleasant*.

In their correspondence, quoted by Sir Rupert Hart-Davis in his valuable edition of Beerbohm notices *More Theatres* (1893–1903), the happy transfer is described. Much later, in 1930, Max explained that the necessity to write every week, walking, as he said, on 'the hebdomadal tight-rope', was a salutary discipline. As he put it, the compulsion to provide continually 'a fugitive article for a largish public is no bad thing for a writer inclined, as I was, to precosity. I believe that my way of writing became more chaste through journalism and stronger.'

That was true. In his earlier essays he had indulged his taste for rare and exotic words some of which must have puzzled readers not well grounded in Greek and Latin and needed a lexicon even if they were. He had been addicted to what was called Gongorism, 'an affected type of diction and style introduced into Spanish literature by the poet Gongora y Argote (1561–1607)'. His verbal tricks could be delightful to those with the right educational equipment but he sensibly realised that he was now writing for play-goers who did want news and views of the week's theatrical supply and did not want to have to consult a dictionary to assist translation of his English into theirs. So to the satisfaction of his new proprietor, Lord Hardwicke, and his new editor, Harold Hodge, he continued unimpedibly for twelve years. Then he dismissed himself, degongorised but still the spritely and incomparable essayist. Then, perhaps, with the linguistic chastity acquired, he would have called his tight-rope exercise weekly instead of 'hebdomadal'.

Uzzard

This comes from a constant friend-in-aid where words are concerned. A cousin of his who was in command of a battalion of the Grenadier Guards related that his sergeant-major had asked permission to bring a charge against a guardsman who had called him an improper name. The nature of the insult was naturally requested. The answer came: 'He called me an uzzard, sir.' When asked what that was the reply was, 'Uzzard, sir, bastard, bastard by a bastard out of a bastard.'

To a query about its source I could find no answer. Eric Partridge's two comprehensive dictionaries of slang do not mention this third degree of illegitimacy. Bastard has been an adjective applied to many things hated or corrupted. It was especially used of heavily sweetened wines. A cheap Barsac or a really bad, non-Spanish wine labelled Sherry qualify for the word. In academic circles and mayor's parlours where sherry is the usual refreshment I have tasted some of this stuff which was definitely uzzard.

W

Wick

After I made a minor appearance in a television programme to which much livelier persons contributed, a Yorkshire friend told me in a letter that I was 'looking young, well and wick'. Young I am not; well I was not feeling. What of wick? If it is an adjective meaning vigorous, as I suppose it does,

I could not agree to his favourable opinion. The camera had lied, but I liked the flattering description. I surmise that the dialect adjective may be derived from the wick in the tallow and conveys the reassuring news that life's candle has not yet burned out.

There are wicks to be snuffed and wicks to be lived in. As a termination of town names wick does not have any adjectival significance. The wick-places can be as sweetly rural as the Cotswold Painswick or as grimly urban as Manchester's Ardwick. The word can be lengthened in sound and hardened in quality to wike or wyke. The name of Heckmondwike does not suggest a mild zephyr blowing in its streets or a delicate idleness in its citizens. There is also a softening to wich or wych. This form has a special connection with salt-pits or springs of brine. Hence Northwich, Nantwich and Droitwich. The arthritic who take the saline baths at Droitwich in Worcestershire may emerge feeling comparatively wick in the Yorkshire sense. It is a nice, sharp adjective for a person who manages to have both feet on the ground and to be up on his toes. But I must regard myself as unwickish since, as Yorkshire says of the senile, I am 'living on borrowed time'.

Wood-wandering

The hyphened, alliterative adjective is no doubt an easy trick which a poet of today would disdain to use. Robert Louis Stevenson wrote verses with modest self-depreciation. He had no conception of himself as a poet and was frank about his secondary status on the foothills of Parnassus. But he has pleased many by pleasing himself with his flow of occasional rhymes. The power of the monosyllable he understood. His often quoted, perhaps too much quoted, *Requiem*,

> Under the wide and starry sky

has only five words of two syllables, and those short ones, amid fifty-four of one syllable. Yet he could spread himself when he chose. I find his 'lone, wood-wandering child' a haunting evocation of his boyhood. It follows riverside thoughts

> Up the sun-chequered, devious bed
> To the far-distant, fountain-head.

Simple, you may say. But the greatest have not disdained the simple tune with alliteration added. They have remembered that 'w' has its own magic in the poetry of wind, water and wilderness. There have been many wood-wandering singers.